THE HAMMARSKJÖLD FORUMS

Case Studies
on
The Role of Law
in the
Settlement of International Disputes

THE INTER-AMERICAN SECURITY SYSTEM
AND
THE CUBAN CRISIS

BACKGROUND PAPERS AND PROCEEDINGS
of
THE THIRD HAMMARSKJÖLD FORUM

COVEY OLIVER
Author of the Working Paper

LYMAN M. TONDEL, Jr.
Editor

Published for

THE ASSOCIATION OF THE BAR OF THE CITY OF NEW YORK

by

OCEANA PUBLICATIONS, INC.
DOBBS FERRY, N.Y.
1964

Table of Contents

Part One

THE WORKING PAPER

V

Part Two

A SUMMARY OF THE FORUM PROCEEDINGS

Participants: Abram Chayes, Julio E. Nuñez, Covey Oliver, Frank
Tannenbaum, Francisco Urrutia-Holguín

APPENDICES

VI

THE THIRD HAMMARSKJÖLD FORUM

November 19, 1962

Participants

PROFESSOR COVEY OLIVER
Law School, University of Pennsylvania

ABRAM CHAYES, ESQ.
Legal Adviser to the United States Department of State

JULIO E. NUNEZ, ESQ.
President, Argentaria S. A. de Finanzas

DR. FRANK TANNENBAUM
*Professor Emeritus of Latin-American History,
Columbia University*

H. E. FRANCISCO URRUTIA-HOLGUIN OF COLOMBIA
*Representative of the United Nations High Commissioner's
Office for Refugees in Latin America*

EDITOR'S FOREWORD

In 1960-61 The Association of the Bar of the City of New York was forcefully reminded by two of its senior members, James N. Rosenberg and Grenville Clark, that it should be devoting more of its resources and attention to the cause of world peace through law. It was not that it had by any means defaulted in this field of law, but rather that none of its existing committees or activities was intended to concentrate on the primary challenge to lawyers in our day—namely, the role of law in the settlement of international disputes.

After exploring numerous possibilities it was concluded to conduct, as forums, a series of case studies. It was deliberately decided to consider disputes of the first magnitude, involving political, military, economic and social, as well as legal, problems. It was understood that existing law might be found to play a minor role in these controversies. Yet it was felt that the role of law, whatever it might be, should be more fully appreciated because if there is to be meaningful progress towards international disarmament and the elimination of war as a means of settling international disputes, then means of settlement alternate to war—means under law—must be developed.

It was recognized that under the spur of ever more devastating weapons, there have been in the last 70 years a series of significant steps in the development of peaceful means for settling international controversies—including the Hague Conventions; the League of Nations and the Permanent Court of International Justice; the United Nations and the International Court of Justice; the Organization of American States; and the Court of Justice of the European Economic Community. These steps have not, however, prevented war. In this sense they have all failed.

Yet, in a larger sense, these efforts may not have failed. World law may be impractical, or impossible of achievement at this stage of human history, but these steps and others may have marked the way towards some of the elements of a world at peace under law. They certainly have reflected, and helped induce, a far more extensive consideration of the problems of peacefully settling international disputes than ever before. And they have had results that should be more generally known. For example, in only one adversary case decided by the Permanent Court of International Justice or the International Court of Justice has the losing nation failed to abide by the Court's decision; and all of the rulings of the Court of Justice of the European Economic Community, many of which have involved economic matters of major concern to the disputants, have been carried out. The United Nations has prevented wars. There has, through all this, been a sort of common law development of the means of peaceful settlement of international disputes even though wars and rumors of war still fill the air.

Accordingly it was concluded that it might be useful, and should surely be educational, for there to be a series of case studies in the role of law in settling international disputes, and three forums were held in 1962 at the House of the Association in New York City. A fourth was held in April, 1963, and a fifth is in the planning stage as this is written. The first considered the Berlin-German crisis; the second, the United Nations action in the Congo; the third, the Cuban crisis of October, 1962; and the fourth, Disarmament. The four volumes of this series are on these four subjects. Each volume contains (1) an outstanding Working Paper, prepared by a prominent legal scholar in the field, which summarizes, but with appropriate detail, the legal and factual background of the dispute; (2) a condensation of the discussion at the Forum by the author of the Working Paper and commentators who included leading participants in the affairs discussed; and (3) an extensive bibliography prepared by the Research Staff of the Association's Library. Due to the unique access of the Association to the United Nations, to national leaders, and to prominent legal scholars, the participants have been notable.

As previously indicated, it was recognized in planning this series that such major disputes as those in Berlin, the Congo and Cuba, and that regarding disarmament and arms control, could not, in practice, be solved exclusively under existing legal methods and that, in any event, rights and duties under law comprised only part of the problem in each case. Yet it clearly appeared at the Forums that the nations involved did have legal rights and duties; that even the Soviet Union seeks to justify, and with great particularity, its actions in the name of law and, for all we know, may even have rejected some courses of action for which even their apologists could not rationalize any legal justification; that rules, or at least patterns, of conduct by nations, by groups of nations, and by the United Nations, are being constantly developed, as in the Congo and in the Inter-American system; and that the experience being acquired in peacefully trying to solve these disputes must be understood if progress is to be made.

If, as we must hope, fear of nuclear devastation is to drive the nations into finding means of peacefully solving controversies with each other, the search for such means can only be hastened by greater undersanding of what actions, ambitions, needs or ideologies lead to critical disputes; of what procedures and devices have helped solve such disputes, and what have not; of what new law is evolving in connection with efforts to solve such disputes; of the extent to which rulers have had regard for at least the pretext of legality; and of what sanctions and obligations have restrained them the most.

In addition to inspiring this series of Forums, James N. Rosenberg of the New York Bar made a substantial financial contribution which enabled the Association to embark on the project. A grant was made by the Ford Foundation early in 1963 to enable the series to continue, and a portion of the earlier cost was met by a grant from the Ottinger Foundation, Inc.

As the original planning of this series neared completion, Dag Hammarskjöld, an honorary member of the Association, was tragically killed in the course of a mission of peace. As a memorial to him the series was entitled "The Hammarskjöld Forums." Adlai E. Stevenson, United States Permanent Representative to the United Nations, and his Deputy, Francis T. P. Plimpton, inaugurated the Forums at the first meeting which was devoted to a consideration of the Berlin-German crisis. Remarks made by them on that occasion are included in Volume I.

In publishing these volumes it is hoped by the Association that each will provide some of those who conduct public discussions, as well as some students and teachers, with background information on a specific controversy; that each will alert the reader to the existing and developing law involved in the particular controversy; and that all who read may thereby become more aware that only by the substitution of the rule of law may war be eliminated as the ultimate means of settling international disputes.

Lyman M. Tondel, Jr.

XI

PART ONE
THE WORKING PAPER

WORKING PAPER: THE INTER-AMERICAN SECURITY SYSTEM AND THE CUBAN CRISIS*

COVEY OLIVER

Professor of Law, University of Pennsylvania

INTRODUCTION

Is this now merely an observation that belongs to history?

> *"We of the United States are prone to assume that since the members of the OAS are solemnly pledged to resist the common enemy, international Communism, and since we regard this threat as greater than all else, this problem should have priority over all else. Consequently we are disappointed and even scandalized when we learn that the Latins do not accept our assessment of the Communist danger. Not only do they regard their own dictatorships as rating more immediate attention, but they regard interventionism itself as a greater evil than Communism."* [1]

The United States and the Latin-American countries are bound together in a security arrangement that is based upon international agreements of an organic or constitutional order. These arrangements state common goals and interests, lay down rules of conduct for the states parties to them, and create institutions to be used by the parties in reaching group decisions upon specific

---

* This paper was written by Professor Covey Oliver of The Law School of the University of Pennsylvania. It was planned and virtually completed prior to the events that began with President Kennedy's address the evening of October 22, 1962. Except for minor changes the original draft has been kept down to heading III-C. The treatment of the Cuban problem under heading III-C has been rewritten to take into account later events, especially the action of the Organization of American States taken on October 23, 1962, and to dispose more summarily than originally had been intended with the developments at the San Jose and Punta del Este meetings of the Organ of Consultation with regard to the Cuban problem. Part IV has been completely rewritten.

problems or issues. The Organization of American States is the principal instrumentality that the United States and her sister republics have created for the execution of these agreements, and they and it are in a legal and organizational relationship with the United Nations. The inter-American system is a legal as well as a political association of states. The organized inter-American system is of comparatively recent origin, but its roots are in the common history of the nations of the New World from the beginnings of their independence. The system is now in crisis, and the crisis involves problems that were not foreseen and provided for when the relevant legal arrangements were made. In the formation of responsible opinion as to provident and effective responses to the challenge of this crisis the aid of lawyers as citizens, as decision-makers, and as counselors to public discourse is greatly needed.

I. THE EVOLUTION OF THE INTER-AMERICAN SYSTEM

A. *From the Latin-American Revolutions (1810-20) through the Roosevelt Corollary*

The idea of an inter-American system of states grew from the common history of revolution of the peoples of this hemisphere against the European powers that colonized it. Until roughly the time of World War II the United States and the Latin-American states were mainly linked by this association, although for the Latin-American states themselves Bolívar and others had the dream of a higher and more definite level of organization.[2] In the initial period the multipartite relationships of the United States with Latin-America were largely cultural and (increasingly with time) economic and social. In this period the United States acted unilaterally in matters of international politics and security involving the hemisphere; and, entirely consistently with the practices of states in that period, the United States made its decisions, including those involving use of force, strictly in the light of its national interests as judged by it. The Monroe Doctrine was a unilateral political pronouncement made to serve the United States' national interests of security from European-based power centers and of freedom to expand, westward, at least. From 1823 to 1945 there was no need even to consider the "legality" of the doctrine, for the law of the times left the United States free to use its power as it liked. The famous dictum of Secretary of State Olney,[3] despite its use of the term "law", does not affect this conclusion; but it does give a sharp picture of the unilateral character of the doctrine as it was being asserted in 1895.

The Corollary, announced by President Theodore Roosevelt in 1905, broadened the scope of the Monroe Doctrine from that of fending off new European adventures in colonialism[4] to the exercise of authority by the United States within the territory of Latin-American states in order to insure that the rights under international law of extra-continental states be provided for without any necessity of their intervention or use of force in this hemisphere. The Corollary, too, was unilateral, political, and "legal", in the sense that there was no law or international agreement against it. Under the Corollary the United States became, until the last marine left Haiti in 1934, the self-appointed "Policeman of the West."[5] On the whole the policeman's intentions were good; sound administration, order, respect for rights under international law (including those of Americans), and improvement were the goals. But, as is said in song to be the lot of even non self-appointed policemen, the lot of the United States was not a happy one, at least in terms of the strong, persistent, and emotional objections of the Latin-American peoples to *Intervention*.

During the latter part of the period under consideration the United States pursued a policy in respect of the long (1910-1919) Mexican Revolution, so well recorded by Dr. Tannenbaum, that from the hindsight of history has had, and continues to have, very serious consequences. In this case the overwhelming power of the United States was involved not only in armed interventions in Mexico, but also in the matter of recognition of governments. First, recognition of a revolutionary regime was withheld because it came to power in an unconstitutional manner; later, when there was no question as to the success of another regime, one that is the direct political ancestor of the Mexican government of today, we exacted undertakings[6] in favor of United States interests that were granted during the Diaz dictatorship in conformity with his law of subsurface rights but contrary to the ancient land law inherited from Spain and re-enacted in the Constitution of 1917. Interventionism as a concept to be resisted and to be controlled by law was broadened, in the Latin-American mind, from the sending of forces to include other uses of power by the United States.

Resistance to intervention in the broad sense is, of course, resistance to United States dominance and even leadership, including dominance or insistent leadership in group decision-making and group action. These are political and socio-psychological facts that bear upon many aspects of our problem and underlie legal provisions we shall examine.

B. *International Undertakings from Montevideo (1933) to Chapultepec (1945)*

The movement toward legal control of dominant power, the United States participating, began with the internal policy deci-

4

sion of the United States to abandon the Roosevelt Corollary. This event has earlier beginnings; but it is marked in history by the preparation of the J. Reuben Clark Memorandum, dated December 17, 1928. The thrust of the memorandum has been described by Dexter Perkins, the leading authority on the history of the Monroe Doctrine:

> ". . . Thus, in a manner more specific than that of Mr. Hughes in 1923, the Clark memorandum sought to divorce Monroeism from the idea of intervention and, in its own words, 'relieve the Doctrine from many of the criticisms which have been aimed against it." [7]

The substance of the Clark Memorandum was communicated to the other American republics by the incoming Hoover Administration in 1928, largely at the initiative of Henry L. Stimson, the father of the policy of the "good neighbor." Thereafter, Perkins writes:

> ". . . by June of 1930, the Roosevelt Corollary had been definitely and specifically repudiated; and since that time there has been no scholarly foundation for the proposition that the Monroe Doctrine as officially interpreted either makes necessary or even tolerates interventions in the affairs of the other states of the New World. The United States had not renounced the right of intervention, but it gave notice that it no longer intended to rest this right upon the principles of 1823." [8]

At the Seventh International Conference of American States, at Montevideo, 1933,[9] the political objectives of the Latin-American States with respect to intervention and recognition were incorporated into an international agreement to which the United States is a party. Pertinent provisions of the Convention on the Rights and Duties of States follow:

> "*Article IV*. States are juridically equal, enjoy the same rights, and have equal capacity in their exercise. The rights of each one do not depend upon the power which it possesses to assure its exercise, but upon the simple fact of its existence as a person under international law.

> "*Article VI*. The recognition of a state [10] merely signifies that the state which recognizes it accepts the personality of the other with all the rights and duties determined by international law. Recognition is unconditional and irrevocable.

5

"Article VIII. No state has the right to intervene in the internal or external affairs of another.

"Article IX. . . . foreigners may not claim rights other or more extensive than those of nationals.

"Article XI. The contracting states definitely establish as the rule of their conduct the precise obligation not to recognize territorial acquisitions or special advantages which have been obtained by force whether this consists in the employment of arms, in threatening diplomatic representations, or in any other effective coercive measure. The territory of a state is inviolable and may not be the object of military occupation nor of other measures of force imposed by another state directly or indirectly or for any motive whatever, even temporarily."

This was an international agreement, not a mere declaration. Some of its provisions have been blurred by later treaty developments, but Article VIII, cast in even more specific language, is now Article 15 of the Charter of the Organization of American States.

Montevideo also took some very tentative steps toward hemispheric security. The Outline accompanying this paper sketches developments along these lines as war came closer in Europe, and after war came to Europe, and finally, when it came to the Americas. Here it is only necessary to emphasize that the United States was the rather quiet but insistent leader in moving the twenty-one nations toward collective security as World War II approached and that the steps taken, though often hesitant, pre-cast the form of the regional security system now in being. For example: At Lima in 1936[11] the pattern, since followed, of required consultation by all the states prior to collective measures of defense, was set. At Panama in 1939[12] the institution of consultation at the foreign ministers' level began. Also, then a high seas neutrality zone around the Americas was asserted against the European belligerents and enforcement of it by national naval units was authorized; and, for the first time, the Latin-American states joined with the United States to provide against transfer of any territory in the Americas between non-American powers.

At their second meeting at Habana in 1940[13] the Foreign Ministers signed a treaty on the provisional administration of European colonies and possessions in the Americas and agreed to two Resolutions of importance here. One, Resolution XV, was the first collective measure specifically directed against external agression and was cast in the now familiar OAS, NATO, etc., patterns of "an attack on one is an attack on all." But no defensive force in being was set up. The organization of cooperation for defense was left for later negotiation, and the occasion of an aggression merely required consultations. Another Resolution recommended that a stand-by committee be created by the Governing Board of the Pan American Union, composed of representatives of five states and to have the duty:

"... of keeping constant vigilance to insure that states between which any dispute exists or may arise, of any nature whatsoever, may solve it as quickly as possible, and of suggesting, without detriment to the methods to be adopted by the parties or to the procedures which they may agree upon, the measures and steps which may be conducive to a settlement."

The committee was also charged to make reports to each meeting of the ministers of foreign affairs and to each international conference of American states regarding ". . . the status of such conflicts and the steps which may have been taken to bring about a solution." From this beginning came the Inter-American Peace Committee that since has had important roles to play, as in the Guatemalan crisis of 1954 when the prior referral to it of the charge of Honduran invasion resulted in the Security Council's withdrawal from the case, despite Soviet objections.

1942-45 were years of close economic and (except for Argentina) political cooperation between the United States and Latin America. In the main the Latin American countries aided or tolerated, albeit sometimes with reluctance, economic warfare and other measures taken against Axis sympathizers by the United States. Some declared war; Brazil and Mexico were active belligerents; and the group, but for the objections of Argentina and Chile, would have voted to break relations with the Axis Powers, rather than (as was done at Rio in 1942) merely[14] to recommend this course. The Inter-American Defense Board and the Inter-American Juridical Committee were established for wartime purposes, and much multilateral activity aided the extensive bilateral arrangements, including lend-lease aid, made between the United States and various ones of her neighbors. The Inter-American Defense Board was entirely advisory and was opposed on grounds

7

of sound military administration by the United States armed services, but it performed some functions and has been continued as an institution of the Organization of American States, charged with defense planning for hemispheric security.

C. *The United Nations and the Inter-American System*

The relationships of Latin America to the League of Nations and (in this country) of the Monroe Doctrine to the Lodge reservations fight are of interest and importance historically but not relevant to this sub-topic, except that we should note two interacting influences from the League experience upon the forms the UN and the OAS were to take. One was that of the twenty-one American republics only the United States was never a member of the League. The other was that in the course of President Wilson's effort to get Senate approval he arranged for a new Article 21 on regional security arrangements to be substituted in the Covenant for the original Article 21 on an entirely different matter.[15] This was the first provision in history for a regional arrangement as we know them today (as distinguished from military alliances and the like), and the new Article 21 made it quite clear that regional understandings for keeping the peace were outside League jurisdiction.

By the time the United Nations Charter began to be planned two views on the nature of the new world organization had developed. One was that it should be universal in its jurisdiction and that regional arrangements, if any, were to be subject to its control. The other was that the United Nations should be a co-ordinator of a group of regional structures that were to have primary authority in matters affecting security. Secretary Hull favored the former. Sumner Welles, perhaps reflecting the professional attention that, over the years, had been given to regionalism by American diplomacy shut out of the League, favored the latter. President Franklin D. Roosevelt and Sir Winston Churchill, at least Secretary Hull thought, inclined to favor the position of Mr. Welles. But the Dumbarton Oaks Proposals of the Big Four, when released after having been negotiated in secrecy, revealed that the negotiators had tended to agree with Mr. Hull. The Proposals recognized regional arrangements as appropriate for dealing with clearly regional matters relating to the maintenance of international peace and security, provided such arrangements and their activities were consistent with the purposes and principles of the United Nations (which, it was proposed, would have wide-ranging powers on matters of peaceful settlement of disputes as well as to deal with aggression). Moreover, the Proposals implied that, after reference to the Security Council, particular cases of a regional character could be delegated to regional agencies. Finally:

> "2. The Security Council should, where appropriate, utilize such arrangements or agencies for enforcement action under its authority, but no enforcement action should be taken under regional agencies without the authorization of the Security Council."

If the Proposal sketched sounds familiar, there is a reason; see Articles 52 and 53 of the Charter. But the Proposals contained no Article 51. The Latin-American countries were apprehensive, and they intensified their calls for an Inter-American conference to provide for the continuation of certain of the wartime agreements and of the inter-American system in the postwar era.

The Mexico City Conference on Problems of Peace and War,[16] 1945, resulted; and the Act of Chapultepec recited and re-affirmed the principles of inter-American international law declared by previous conferences, including the "act against one is an act against all" principle and the requirement of consultation. The Act of Chapultepec also attempted a general definition of aggression:

> "3. That every attack of a State against the integrity or the inviolability of the territory, or against the sovereignty or political independence of an American State, shall, conformably to Part III hereof, be considered as an act of aggression against the other States which sign this Act. In any case invasion by armed forces of one State into the territory of another trespassing boundaries established by treaty and demarcated in accordance therewith shall constitute an act of aggression."

With the first sentence, compare Article 2-4 of the United Nations Charter. The second sentence anticipated the concept of aggression that so far has been used by the United Nations. It is interesting to note that refinements on definition of the sort that have been attempted in various attempts to codify the crime of aggression, such as economic pressure and the outfitting of

9

armed bands, were not included in the Chapultepec formulation.

The Act then went on to a declaration that in the event of aggression the parties would consult ". . . in order to agree upon the measures it may be advisable to take." The Act further provided for the interim continuation of the institutions of mutual security for the duration of the war and until the establishment of a new security arrangement for the postwar. As to the new organization:

> ". . . for the purpose of meeting threats or acts of aggression against any American Republic following the establishment of peace, the Governments of the American Republics consider the conclusion, in accordance with their constitutional processes, of a treaty establishing procedures whereby such threats or acts may be met by the use, by all or some of the signatories of said treaty, of any one or more of the following measures: recall of chiefs of diplomatic missions; breaking of diplomatic relations; breaking of consular relations; breaking of postal, telegraphic, telephonic, radio-telephonic relations; interruption of economic, commercial and financial relations; use of armed force to prevent or repel aggression."

On the face of it, the Act did not seem quite to fit the Dumbarton Oaks Proposals.

The Act specified that the anti-aggression Declaration and the above-quoted Recommendation constitute a "regional arrangement for dealing with such matters relating to the maintenance of international peace and security as are appropriate for regional action in this Hemisphere."

After Chapultepec came the organizing conference on the United Nations at San Francisco. The Latin Americans had deferred at Chapultepec to a United States wish not to be too tightly committed prior to the San Francisco meeting and did not push there a resolution favoring autonomy for the inter-American system; but their observations on the Dumbarton Oaks proposals, submitted at San Francisco, made it clear that they wanted at least priority, if not autonomy, in the settlement of hemispheric disputes. The Latin-American position brought about one of the major crisis of the San Francisco meeting. The impasse was resolved by a compromise proposed by Senator Arthur Vandenberg:

> "The right of self-defense is inherent in every nation-state. In the event of an attack against any one of a group of countries

which have a tradition of mutual assistance, such as expressed in the principles and objectives of an arrangement such as the Act of Chapultepec, then states may take concerted action against an attack on any one of them. This right shall not, however, deny to the Security Council the right to take any action it deems necessary to maintain international peace and security."

This, essentially, is Article 51 of the Charter, but with this impor-tant difference: Senator Vandenberg's proposal could be read to imply that the Security Council might supersede by its decision to discuss the situation a regional organization acting defensively. Article 51 makes it clear that until the Security Council "has taken the measures necessary to maintain international peace and security," defensive operations through a regional arrangement may continue. As to jurisdiction, the Charter establishes the relationships of the Security Council to a regional organization in being as follows:

(i) *As to peaceful measures of settlement* [Chapter VI]: Jurisdiction is concurrent, but the Security Council is obliged to encourage exercise of jurisdiction by the regional arrangement. [Article 52-3]

(ii) *As to self-defense* [Chapter VII]: Jurisdiction as to response to or consideration of the act of aggression is concurrent, but the regional arrangement is privileged to take defensive measures, including the use of force, against an overt act of aggression without authorization from the Security Council. Such defensive action does not bar the Security Council from considering the problem, and the regional arrangement must immediately inform the Security Council of its actions. But until the Security Council acts [at least by a vote to act, but most likely actual steps will be required] the regional arrangement can continue to act. [Article 51]

(iii) *Enforcement action against threats to the peace, breaches of the peace, and acts of aggression* [Chapter VII]: United Nations jurisdiction is exclusive, but a regional arrangement may be authorized or instructed to take enforcement action as an agent of the United Nations. [Article 53-1]

Later herein we shall consider these jurisdictional interrelation-ships in connection with current security problems of the Western Hemisphere. Suffice it here to generalize that self-defense is authorized against an overt act of aggression as, for example, an

11

invasion or other action coming within the Chapultepec definition. Hostile and threatening conduct short of aggression may constitute threats to peace or even breaches of the peace; but such security dangers do not, in Charter terms, fall to regional organizations to redress by use of force. As is well known, unilateral use of force to forestall an anticipated threat to peace or breach of peace has come to be called "preventive war," in most circles a pejorative term connoting illegality as well as folly. Whether such action if taken by a regional arrangement, legally having no greater authority in the premises, would merit or receive a more tolerant label, such as "anticipatory collective self-defense" is a question that cannot be answered fully today.

II. THE ORGANIZATION OF AMERICAN STATES ESTABLISHED: LEGAL ASPECTS

The Vandenberg Compromise was accepted by the Latin-American states at San Francisco on the understanding that the twenty-one would meet as soon as convenient to provide a permanent normative and organizational structure for inter-American security. The steps taken in implementation of this understanding are contained in the two international agreements sketched in the Outline. Commentary here will be directed to tracing into the new arrangements ideas and institutions that previously had been developed and to pointing up innovations and shifts in emphasis.

A. *The Inter-American Treaty of Reciprocal Assistance, Rio de Janeiro, 1947*[17]

The Rio Pact fixes the principles that are to govern the inter-American community when its security is threatened. It does not provide new organs of action or for an infrastructure. It does specify that the Organ of Consultation shall be the foreign ministers of the members, that a consultative meeting may be called by a simple majority of members, that decisions of the Organ shall be by two-thirds vote, and that a quorum shall be the same number required for a vote. There is no veto and no provision for the expulsion or suspension of a member. The Agreement is replete almost to the point of redundancy with assertions requiring congruity with the United Nations Charter. The definition of aggression is the same as that of Chapultepec, except that invasion of territory includes territory that is under the effective jurisdiction of another state and there is added:

> "a. Unprovoked armed attack by a State against the territory, the people, or the land, sea or air forces of another State." [18]

Any armed attack on an American state within the geographic region described in the treaty (all the Western Hemisphere, including Canada and Greenland, wide areas of ocean approaches,

and a sector of Antarctica) requires each member to assist the member attacked by such measures as it may determine upon ". . . in accordance with the principle of continental solidarity." The Organ of Consultation shall meet to provide collective measures. [Article 3]

Any aggression other than an armed attack is dealt with by a required consultation, and such aggression is defined as:

> "*Article 6.* If the inviolability or the integrity of the territory or the political independence of any American State should be affected by an aggression which is not an armed attack or by an extra-continental or intra-continental[19] conflict, or by any other fact or situation that might endanger the peace of America . . ."

Article 7 deals with conflicts between two or more American states and declares that, without prejudice to the right of self-defense under Article 51 of the United Nations Charter, the parties in consultation shall call for the suspension of hostilities and the restoration of the *status quo ante bellum,* and:

> ". . . shall take in addition all other necessary measures to re-establish or maintain inter-American peace and security and for the solution of the conflict by peaceful means. The rejection of the pacifying action will be considered in the determination of the aggressor and in the application of the measures which the consultative meeting may agree upon."

The measures that for the purposes of the Treaty the parties may agree upon under Article 8 are the same as those specified at Chapultepec, including use of armed force. The careful integration of the arrangement into the United Nations Charter and the drafting of Article 7 (characterizing it as one on peaceful settlement) preclude the implication that armed force could be used under Article 7 to enforce a peaceful settlement proposed by the Organ of Consultation.

B. *The Charter of the Organization of American States, Bogotá, 1948*[20]

The Charter of the Organization of American States contains normative provisions, and it is these that are mainly important

14

to us here. But it also creates an international organization, an entity with international legal personality. The civics of this organization can best be presented for our purposes by a chart. One is provided in Appendix B.

The Organization has a permanent Secretariat, the Pan American Union, and a permanent representative group, the Council of the Organization. The Council has certain supervisory functions and performs tasks assigned by the Inter-American Conference (the periodic meetings of the American states) and the Organ of Consultation (the foreign ministers). Also, it is a stand-by organization for emergencies whose chairman (elected each year and who cannot succeed himself) has the power to call a meeting of the Organ of Consultation, as well as of the Council, in case of an armed attack within the territory of an American state or within the geographic region delimited by the Rio Pact.

The Organization has many functions other than defense, as a glance at Appendix B will show. Cultural, welfare, economic, social, and legal matters are provided for. Although we are primarily concerned with the legal aspects of security problems, it should not be forgotten that these other aspects of our relations with Latin America are of vital importance and that institutions for dealing with them have been developed and are functioning, frequently with great effectiveness.

In contrast with the North Atlantic Treaty Organization there is no force in being assigned to the Organization, and the military experts are in staff, not line, assignments. In contrast with the United Nations, it has a General Assembly but no Security Council, no court. The Secretariat, although permanent, has functions similar to those of the conventional secretariat appointed for an international conference. This contrasts with the duties and powers of the Secretary-General of the United Nations as specified in Article 99 of the Charter and as they have evolved.

Passing to the normative provisions of the Charter, in Chapter II there is enumerated a set of principles that the American states "reaffirm." These principles include some that state standards of conduct required by international law, but others involve matters not governed by international law and ordinarily thought of as falling within the exclusive competence of individual states, such as:

15

"d)   The solidarity of the American States and the high aims which are sought through it requires the political organization of those States on the basis of the effective exercise of representative democracy.

"h)   Social justice and social security are the bases of lasting peace.

"l)   The education of peoples should be directed toward justice, freedom, and peace."

There is no suggestion elsewhere in the OAS Charter, or in the Rio Pact, that any of the Principles of Chapter II, including *d)* above, could be *per se* the basis of any legal demand or action against a member not living up to them. Thus, as would also appear from the bases that have been stated for actions that have been taken against dictatorships, as in the case of Trujillo, departures from the Principles must be susceptible of characterization as a threat to peace in the Americas before the measures specified in Article 8 of the Rio Pact may be taken, and even then, for reasons previously given, use of armed force would not be authorized.

An additional reason might be found in the interdiction of intervention and the insistence upon sovereignty over internal affairs specified in Chapter III, dealing with the fundamental rights and duties of states. This Chapter goes over the same ground as was covered at the Montevideo Conference of 1933, and, in the main, deals with the fundamental rights and duties of states similarly, although there are a few intriguing differences[21] not relevant here. Articles 15 and 16, quoted at pages 58-59, are very sweeping. Taking them together, they seem to denounce collective, as well as individual, state pressures on a state, even as to its external affairs that affront or threaten the security of other states.

Just how the sweep of these articles can be squared juridically with the powers of the Organization under Article 8 of the Rio Pact in cases where the policy of a state is such as to bring about a threat to peace or to threaten the security of other states is worthy of reflection. Some may be inclined to parse Article 15 and conclude that measures taken in the situation suggested above are not objectionable if they are not intended or motivated by designs on the personality or the territorial integrity or political independence of the state, as some have argued (under Article 2-4 of the United Nations Charter) in defense of the British-French action at Suez.[22] Others may say (and I suspect some diplomats think it) that Articles 15 and 16 are, after all, merely hortatory and without significant political or legal effect. One rejoinder might be: "Do you mean to say that a violation of the rights of a state as declared in the Bogotá Charter is not a violation of the Charter?" The practical lawyer or diplomat might well conclude that, while these sections may not forbid economic or other non-force pressure on a state because of its conduct, their sweep is a serious obstacle to getting a two-thirds vote in the Organization favorable to such a course. Surely, however, these sections cannot be taken to imply that United Nations measures authorized by the Charter would be in violation of the rules of a regional arrangement that is repeatedly declared in its own organic acts to be subordinate to the United Nations.

III. THE ESTABLISHED INTER-AMERICAN SYSTEM AND THE THREAT OF SINO-SOVIET INTRUSION

In the period leading up to World War II, as we have seen, the United States saw the dangers to itself and to the Western Hemisphere as early as 1936 and began to try to move its sister republics toward organizing against Axis infiltration. The response was slow, reluctant, and partial—until war came. In part this was caused by the opposition of a few, but important, Latin-American countries. In major part it resulted from the belief of Latins that the United States was unduly apprehensive about the reality of axis infiltration and subversion. The United States had its eye on the large German, Italian, and Japanese ethnic groups living in various Latin-American countries, in many instances with very strong positions in the internal economies; it believed that Pan-Germanism was a clear and present danger and that Japanese everywhere kept a residual loyalty to the Emperor. The Latins were not impressed because of the success of the local Germans in fitting themselves into the societies of the countries in which they lived and the quiet industriousness of the Japanese. The United States did not seem to be greatly concerned about the Italians, but it is probable that the continued resistance of Argentina to our efforts may have been to some degree caused by the complete integration in that country, to the point even of affecting the Spanish language as spoken there, of very substantial Italian stocks. Our fears were not so much that the Nazi-Fascist ideology would be transplanted to the Americas but that Germans and Japanese living in Latin America would engage in sabotage, propaganda, espionage, and related activities on behalf of the Axis. When war came to the Americas, control devices to deal with such activities were worked out, and the Latin Americans, in the main, helped in dealing with these threats. Also, they joined with us in preventive measures against possible Axis take-over of Western Hemisphere territories of the countries the Axis had conquered, or threatened to conquer.

The combined efforts against Axis subversives actually turned up little to justify United States fears, and with the complete

18

defeat of the Axis the idea developed that the United States had been too nervous about the threat. This attitude was certainly involved in Latin-American appraisals of the United States' fears about Sino-Soviet intrusions prior to October 23, 1962: *"Los gringos faltan de sangre fría; los norteamericanos más que los elefantes tienen miedo de ratoncillos."* [23] This attitude was reinforced by the fears of internal communism publicized in the McCarthy era. Until the events of October, 1962, the United States had not been able to convince the Latin Americans that our major concern as to "hemispheric communism" is not espionage and the like but the establishment of Sino-Soviet political and military power in being in the Western Hemisphere. A further complication, of course, is the influence of doctrinal Marxism on some intellectuals and demagogic leaders in various Latin-American countries. Many of these, most observers agree, are not the dispatched agents of Moscow but are economic and historical determinists (who to my way of thinking misinterpret the causes and incorrectly prescribe the remedies for the economic and social distress of their countries). But until the case of Sino-Soviet intrusion was established, United States efforts were seen, not as genuinely based in concern for the security of the hemisphere, but as an ideological counter-attack in which we were trying to induce our neighbors to join. These generalizations, perhaps, are beyond my province as your reporter on the law; but I also have a very minor competence in Latin-American political sociology and was involved in the World War II anti-Axis effort. At any rate, it is my opinion that the apathy with which the Latin-American states responded to United States initiatives prior to October 23, 1962 had its roots in what I have just summarized, even though their doubts and objections may have been expressed formally in "juridical" terms.

A. *The Caracas Declaration, March 13, 1954*

The freedom and encouragement given to Communist groups in Guatemala by the Arbenz regime and reports of arms shipments to that country aroused the concern of the United States early in 1954. The Tenth Inter-American Conference[24] met at Caracas on March 1, and Secretary of State Dulles made a determined drive, in a generally apathetic atmosphere and with strong support only from six countries under dictatorships, to get a declaration of common opposition to "the international communist movement." There had been a general resolution at the Ninth Conference (1948)[25] that international communism was incompatible with the concept of American freedom and a danger to the American States; but Mr. Dulles' objective, at Caracas, as he stated it, was not mere reaffirmation of the earlier resolution but a further declaration that ". . . domination and control of the political institutions of any American State by the international Communist movement would constitute intervention by a foreign political power and be a threat to the peace of America."[26] In a later statement, Mr. Dulles explained in answer to a taunting question from the Guatemalan Foreign Minister that "international communism" is ". . . that far-flung clandestine political organization which is operated by the leaders of the Communist Party of the Soviet Union . . . It . . . is not a theory, not a doctrine, but an aggressive, tough, political force, backed by great resources, and serving the most ruthless empire of modern times."

Farther on in the same address to the Politico-Juridical Committee of the Conference, Mr. Dulles referred to that portion of the Monroe Doctrine that spoke of the dangers that would come if ". . . the Allied Powers should extend their political system to any portion of either continent . . . ," and declared that in this respect the Monroe Doctrine ". . . had long since ceased to be merely unilateral."

The Declaration of Caracas was passed by the Politico-Juridical Committee[27] by a vote of 17-1 (Guatemala), with Mexico and Argentina abstaining. Its operative clauses are carried in the Outline (p. 59). In addition to the principles announced, the Declaration contained two recommendations: (i) measures to be taken in each state to detect the activities of the international communist movement and its sources of funds and (ii) for exchange of information between the governments on subversive activities. The United States draft of the operative clause had read that the danger "would call for appropriate action under existing treaties." The language "would call for consultation to consider the adoption of measures in accordance with existing treaties" [see Outline] comes from an amendment introduced by Colombia. The reassurance regarding non-intervention was proposed by Mr.

Dulles during the Conference and is carried in the official record as a "Recommendation," although, quite clearly, it relates to the substance of the operative clause.

The juridical standing of this Declaration is far from clear,[28] but, at least, it is a political commitment to consult to consider collective measures when the extension of the political system of an extra-continental power threatens. If the Monroe Doctrine was "Pan-Americanized" at Caracas as expert Latin Americanists[29] say, just what was it that was Pan-Americanized? If the Monroe Doctrine was originally a unilateral political doctrine, its multipartite version is arguably also only a statement of policy, not a normative principle. Does the adoption of a multipartite policy against external political systems negative the continued existence of the original unilateral policy? My review of the negotiating history at Caracas leads me to the views that the United States did not commit its foreign policy in this matter exclusively to group decisions and that unilateral action not contrary to other commitments, such as those against intervention under the Charter of the Organization of American States and the obligations to the Charter of the United Nations as to unilateral use of force outside the area of self-defense, remains unaffected by the Declaration of Caracas. Admittedly, however, an interpretation that the Declaration contemplates that no unilateral action, except individual self-defense, is to be taken prior to consultation on collective measures is possible.

There are similar uncertainties as to legal effect and intention with regard to the bearing of the Caracas Declaration upon the sweeping interdiction of intervention in the Charter of the Organization of American States. Group, as well as individual state, intervention is there declared to be against the fundamental rights of states, and even collective coercive measures short of armed entry into territory are proscribed. Did Caracas carve out an exception? We cannot be sure from a paper survey, although the atmosphere of the Caracas Conference strongly suggests that the Latin-American representatives did not intend to commit their countries to any reversal of the rule against intervention, but merely expressed willingness to consult as to measures that could as plausibly as not be characterized as amounting to intervention under Articles 15 and 16. The Colombian amendment described above supports this conclusion, as do also the positions taken by various delegations at the San Jose and Punta del Este meetings of the Foreign Ministers on the Cuban problem, later to be discussed herein.

Measures taken against an American state under the Caracas Declaration, whether by another American state or by the inter-American group, would undoubtedly now[30] raise issues under the United Nations Charter. If the result of such measures could by any reasonable possibility be characterized as a "dispute" under Chapter VI[31] or as a "situation"[32] under Chapter VII, the preliminary question in the United Nations would be whether United Nations consideration of the dispute or situation, as the case may be, should be deferred pending efforts at resolution by the regional organization. On this issue the Guatemalan experience and the steps taken so far with respect to Sino-Soviet presence in Cuba must be considered before analysis can be attempted of the legality under the United Nations Charter of particular steps that might be taken to eradicate Sino-Soviet political and military presence in the hemisphere.

B. *Juridical Aspects of the Guatemalan Crisis of 1954*

Within a short time after the adjournment of the Caracas Conference, reports of arms shipments to Guatemala aroused the concern of the United States. Efforts were made to get waivers from various maritime nations outside the Soviet orbit as to high seas visitation and search of vessels flying their flags, but the requests of the United States were rejected. On June 19, 1954, Guatemala referred the matter of an attack from Honduras to the Inter-American Peace Committee; and that body was immediately convened, only to be told by Guatemala the next day that it should suspend action, because also on June 19 the matter had been referred to the Security Council. Thus, for the first time was presented an issue as to whether the regional organization or the Security Council should act.

This issue was debated in the Security Council on the basis of a Brazilian-Colombian resolution that the Security Council should refer the case to the OAS. Guatemala (invited to sit with the Council under Article 32 of the Charter) opposed the resolution on the ground that the case was one of aggression under Chapter VII of the Charter and that it could not be classified as

22

a mere "dispute" as to which the OAS should be given primary competence under Parts VI (Pacific Settlement of Disputes) and VIII (Regional Arrangements). The Soviet delegate vigorously supported Guatemala and contributed his share to a bitter verbal duel with the representative of the United States after the latter had reacted adversely to Soviet intrusion into a hemisphere matter.[33] [See Outline, *infra,* p. 61]

The Soviet Union vetoed the Brazilian-Colombian proposal, and the Security Council ultimately voted (unanimously) a "let there be no further bloodshed"[34] resolution introduced by France. This resolution, the Soviet delegate insisted, was important, because it showed that the Security Council did have jurisdiction over threats to peace in the Western Hemisphere and could take up this case again if need be. Other delegations tended to shrug off the resolution of an event of little consequence and to turn to the Inter-American Peace Committee for action. However, before a sub-committee of that body could make a report from the scene, the Arbenz regime was displaced by the Castillo Armas regime that had come in from Honduras, with the assistance, it is reported, of defections from the professional military in Guatemala, incensed by Arbenz's plan to arm a non-professional, "popular" militia.[35] This development closed the case; the plaintiff had disappeared while the modalities of settlement were going on.

In Latin America it was suspected that the United States had, at the least, made the coup possible by the supply (or permitting the supply) of American aircraft and arms to Guatemala's neighbors. This, together with feelings that it had not been clearly proved that the displaced government was a Soviet instrumentality, gave rise to public expressions of frustration and cynicism in Latin America as to (i) the genuineness of the United States' renunciation of non-intervention and (ii) the effectiveness of the anti-aggression machinery of the UN Charter and the OAS. These attitudes, undoubtedly, gave rise to some of the Latin-American doubts in the matter of Cuba, particularly after the sad affair at the Bahía de los Cochinos.

C. *Cuba, 1960—October?, 1962: The Problem of Proof*

In view of the action taken by the Organization of American States on October 23, 1962, the review here of the earlier efforts of the United States (at San José,[36] at Punta del Este,[37] and in conversations at Washington in early October, 1962) to obtain agreement of its OAS partners on a course of action with regard to the Cuban situation need deal only with the major problems that these discussions brought to light. The first and most important was the problem of proof as to the nature and extent of Soviet political and military presence in the Western Hemisphere in association with the Castro regime. Largely for failure of proof sufficient to carry conviction internally in various Latin-American countries, they were willing at San José only to condemn Sino-Soviet efforts to exploit unsettled situations in the hemisphere. They were not willing to censure Cuba. At Punta del Este a similar situation prevailed, but for a smaller group of states. A sharper indictment of the communist offensive in the Americas was drawn, and, by a vote of 20 to 1 (Cuba), the present government of Cuba was found to be identified with the Sino-Soviet bloc and hence disqualified to continue to participate in the work of the Inter-American Defense Board.[38] But a watered-down resolution on the suspension of trade with Cuba received only 16 affirmative votes, with abstentions by Brazil, Chile, Ecuador, and Mexico.[39] Opposition to the exclusion of Castro Cuba from the inter-American system centered on the juridical question whether the Foreign Ministers meeting as the Organ of Consultation have the power under the OAS Charter to exclude a member. As the Charter does not have a provision on suspension or expulsion of members, several delegations took the position that Cuba could be expelled only by the convocation of an inter-American conference to amend the Charter, under Article 111[40] thereof. Mr. Rusk for the United States argued that the Organ of Consultation (at least when the Foreign Ministers, rather than their delegates in the Council, are so serving) is a "plenary body" that can consider and reach agreement on matters of mutual interest. The juridical issue was not settled at Punta del Este, but even its avoidance by a formula based on the concept that ". . . the present government of Cuba has voluntarily placed itself outside the inter-American system"[41] got only a barely sufficient 14 votes, with abstentions by Argentina, Bolivia, Brazil, Chile, Ecuador, and Mexico. The juridical issue did present genuine legal difficulties, and the United States assertion as to the plenary authority of the Organ of Consultation perhaps raised more legal questions than it sought in this context to answer. Nonetheless, the under-

24

lying cause for resistance was the fact that several of the larger countries, such as Brazil, Chile, and Mexico, had not received proof as to the extent of Cuba's defection from the hemisphere sufficient to be politically credible internally, in countries where the Castro regime was still an object of sympathy, or even of hope.

The informal meeting of the OAS Foreign Ministers at Washington, October 2-3, 1962, was held without formal agenda, voting, official minutes, or resolutions, to discuss ". . . the situation in Cuba and other subjects of mutual interest." [42] In view of the state of the record it is not possible to assess here its significance, either in relationship to earlier efforts or to the developments of October 22-23, beyond noting the innovation made by the manner of consultation agreed upon.

IV. THE LAW AND THE CUBAN CRISIS
AFTER OCTOBER 22, 1962

President Kennedy's address to the Nation in the early evening of October 22, 1962, will have a great place in history, if there is to be any history, and the forces and processes it set in motion mark one of this Nation's boldest efforts to insure that this planet continue to have a human history. For us on this occasion the most important aspects of this act of leadership are those that link it carefully to existing international institutions for keeping the peace and to the law. In this context the following are its major points for us here: [43]

> 1. The build-up of offensive missile capabilities in Cuba by the U.S.S.R. was declared to be ". . . an explicit threat to the peace and security of all the Americas, in . . . defiance of the Rio Pact of 1947. . . ."
>
> 2. Self-defense (individual and collective) against guided missiles and nuclear weapons includes measures directed against their presence in situations where such presence is a clear and present danger to other states. Anticipatory self-defense [44] should, however, avoid the use of armed counter-force so long as measures short of it show reasonable promise of removing the threat.
>
> 3. The threat from nuclear-guided missile capability in Cuba is to be dealt with against the state that created it: ". . . It shall be the policy of this nation to regard any nuclear missile launched from Cuba against any nation in the Western Hemisphere as an attack by the Soviet Union on the United States requiring a full retaliatory response upon the Soviet Union."
>
> 4. The Organ of Consultation of the OAS was called into immediate session to deal with the threat to hemispheric security and ". . . to invoke Articles 6 and 8 of the Rio treaty in support of *all necessary action.*" [45] [Although not explicit in the address, the quarantine action announced as United States policy by the President did not go into legal effect until after the OAS had agreed to it as a collective measure on October 23, 1962.]
>
> 5. To the Security Council as a provisional measure under Chapter VII, Article 40, was referred for immediate consideration the dismantling under UN inspection of existing missile

installations in Cuba. [The quarantine, characterized as defensive action by implication in the speech and clearly so treated by the Organ of Consultation, was not referred to the Security Council.]

6. The limited and selective character of quarantine to be put into effect was stressed, but with a reservation of position as to its possible extension if need should arise.

The first international action taken in response to the initiative of the United States was that of the Council of the Organization of American States, meeting as the Organ of Consultation on an emergency basis, as provided in Article 39 of the OAS Charter. The Secretary of State on this occasion represented the United States at the Council. The Organ of Consultation did the following: [46]

1. It found by ". . . incontrovertible evidence . . ." that ". . . Cuba . . . has secretly endangered the peace of the continent [47] by permitting the establishment of intermediate and middle-range missiles on its territory by the Sino-Soviet powers. . . ."

2. It called ". . . for the immediate dismantling and withdrawal from Cuba of all missiles and other weapons with any offensive capability."

3. It recommended ". . . that the member states, in accordance with Articles 6 and 8 of the Inter-American Treaty of Reciprocal Assistance, take all measures, individually and collectively, including the use of armed force, which they may deem necessary to ensure that the government of Cuba cannot continue to receive from the Sino-Soviet powers military material and related supplies which may threaten the peace and security of the continent and to prevent the missiles in Cuba with offensive capability from ever becoming an active threat to the peace and security of the continent. . . ."

4. Decided to inform the Security Council of its action, in accordance with Article 54 of the Charter of the United Nations.

Uruguay's abstention for lack of instructions was later removed following authorization from the collegial presidency of that country; so that the finding of fact, item 2 above, and the portion of 3 that refers to the quarantine have received unanimous approval. Brazil, Mexico and Bolivia abstained on the second portion of item 3, above. The reader is in a position to judge for himself the significance of the OAS action in terms of positive hemispheric association against a common external threat and the precision and attentiveness with which the legal and organizational inter-relationships we have considered were treated. He will note, further, that a residue of reservation about use of force within Cuba remained. Whether this is based upon still lingering fears of Intervention, or arises out of legal problems related to the sweep of the non-intervention provisions of the OAS Charter, or reflects internal situations, or represents foreign policy estimates, or a combination of these, cannot be accurately weighed at this writing.

On Sunday, October 28, 1962, just before another rewriting of this Part began, the office radio that the times require gave the announcement that the Chairman of the Council of Ministers of the U.S.S.R. had declared to President Kennedy the willingness of the Soviet government, without related conditions, to order the dismantling of the missile installations in Cuba and the cessation of arms shipments. There is today HOPE. There comes that pang of fear that some power-shift in the Soviet Union might shatter this feeling of relief and of great expectations for a provident detente, a modus vivendi, or better. But hope overcomes this fear, and we face the future expectantly, knowing that the road to peace is hard, that set-backs will be encountered, and that new difficulties will arise to challenge courage, intelligence, and patience. But in the past few days we have seen man and the institutions for peace and survival he has created respond to grave need and in the process grow. It is better, I believe, to close this text on this note than to attempt now to analyze the problems raised under the remaining headings of the Outline. Many of these, we all hope, will not become again active topics of concern. If we know they could arise and how they relate to what we have studied together, we can, individually, think about them, and if need arises, discuss them in the Forum. At this writing the main thing to note in closing is that our inter-American system and the world's peacekeeping institutions have not been found wanting and that, not having failed, deserve our respect, our loyalty, and our professional comprehension.

PART TWO
THE FORUM

THE FORUM: A SUMMARY OF THE PROCEEDINGS*

I. THE INTER-AMERICAN SECURITY SYSTEM AND THE CUBAN CRISIS—BACKGROUND AND GENERAL CONSIDERATIONS

A. *The Evolution of the Inter-American Security System*

One of the historical bulwarks of the inter-American security system is the Monroe Doctrine. Yet this Doctrine is considered by many historians and others to be merely "a unilateral political pronouncement" made by the United States to serve its own national interests in security from European powers and in freedom to expand westward.

Early in the discussion, Ambassador URRUTIA, from Colombia, presented a different historical explanation of the Monroe Doctrine, stating that the United States' interests were not the only interests involved in its creation. "As you may know", he said, "we took advantage of the Napoleonic wars to start our independence wars. But, when Napoleon was defeated, we faced the problem that the Holy Alliance organized in Vienna decided to help the Spanish King to re-establish his authority in Latin America. In fact, Russia sent troops to Spain that were to join the Spanish battalion with Cabeza de San Juan in 1820, and were embarked to Venezuela.

"Fortunately, the Spanish troops rebelled and, thanks to that, the Russian troops did not arrive in Venezuela. But it was a very close call. We then sent notes to Washington, begging the United States to sign some kind of self-defense treaty with us.

"We couldn't convince them in 1820; we couldn't convince them in 1821. It was only when the United Kingdom asked the United States to join in a protest against Czar Alexander, who had decided to claim one hundred miles of territorial waters of the Bering Strait and to claim Alaska—the first claim in American territory because he also wanted to claim California—that Monroe

---

* This summary was prepared by William D. Zabel of the New York Bar.

31

decided to agree to the Monroe Doctrine. The Monroe Doctrine was unilaterally announced, however, because at the last minute President Monroe decided that he would announce the doctrine alone rather than as a joint doctrine with the United Kingdom as first proposed.

"In fact, the origin of the Monroe Doctrine comes from the common fear of the Latin-American states of the Czar's support of Spain, and of the United States of the Czar's decision to claim Alaska and the Straits of Bering.

"Immediately after the Monroe Doctrine was announced, we invited the United States to internationalize the Doctrine. We wanted the Doctrine to be converted into a self-defense treaty. As you know, the United States Congress agreed; the President was afraid; and the delegates never arrived at the Pan American meeting.

"But from 1823 to the Caracas Conference, what we wanted was a self-defense treaty . . . By the middle of the century, when we were afraid that the European powers were again trying to get too much influence in Latin America and, specifically, that France and Britain wanted to control Panama, then again we came here and asked the United States for protection. We signed the treaty in 1846 as far as Colombia is concerned so that the United States would declare that it would not permit a European power to control Panama.

"In the history of the 1846 treaty, the United States made the commitment—'To guarantee the sovereignty and property rights that Colombia has on the Panama Canal.' Of course we claim that Roosevelt violated the 1846 treaty and, moreover, when he took Panama, he not only violated the 1846 treaty but also the whole idea of a self-defense pact for all the continent which we had sought instead of just a unilateral doctrine as that [the Roosevelt Corollary] was.

"As to the decision to abandon the so-called Roosevelt Corollary, I agree with Professor Oliver that Clark's memorandum was very important.* But Latin Americans considered President Wilson responsible for the change of the whole policy because it was President Wilson in his campaign in 1913 who openly criticized the Roosevelt international policy. That was the beginning of the

---

* See page 5, *supra.*

change in the United States' policy toward its Latin-American neighbors.

"The war in 1914-1918 did not permit President Wilson to take the action he wanted, so we had to wait until Clark's memorandum at the end of the Hoover Administration."

Ambassador URRUTIA indicated that by 1947 the wheel had come full circle and that the Rio Pact, accepted by the Latin-American countries and the United States, was "the treaty on self-defense that we had wanted since 1820, written more or less on the same terms suggested by us in 1820."

After this historic elaboration of the Monroe Doctrine, the discussion progressed without any further reference to the Doctrine. Later, near the end of the discussion, a member of the audience asked whether the Monroe Doctrine was now dead. Professor TANNENBAUM answered that "the Monroe Doctrine has always meant at any given time only what the President said it meant," and suggested "that the unanimous support given to President Kennedy in this crisis, in the attempt to keep a non-American power out of this hemisphere, in some ways finally and permanently makes the Monroe Doctrine a collective American doctrine."

B. *The Creation of the Organization of American States; Its Structure and Functions*

The eventual creation of the collective self-defense organization, which Ambassador URRUTIA said the Latin-American states had sought since 1820, was facilitated by the United Nations Charter and its concept of regional organizations. The Dumbarton Oaks proposals for a United Nations organization contained no clear authorization for regional organizations to use collective self-defense action to protect a member or members. But Article 51 of the United Nations Charter enabled a regional organization to take defensive measures against overt acts of aggression without the authorization of the Security Council.* Prior to the adoption of the United Nations Charter with its Article 51, it was feared that the formation of the United Nations might deter the effective creation of a hemispheric defense pact. Ambassador URRUTIA explained the situation:

---

* See pages 10 -11, *supra*.

"The Dumbarton Oaks proposals were reviewed at Yalta, and what was agreed to at Yalta is disgraceful. What was agreed to at Yalta was this: The Security Council alone could permit the use of armed forces, even in self-defense, and these actions could only be taken by the Security Council within the veto power. This is why, when we were invited to San Francisco, we fought such proposals because if we had had the Cuban crisis under such a charter we couldn't do anything in self-defense, neither the United States nor the OAS, until we got authorization from the Security Council. And we know that such authorization is almost impossible because of the veto power.

"Let's face it. The veto procedure was not a Soviet proposal; it was a United States proposal to overcome the problems faced by Wilson with the U.S. Senate in 1918 which prevented him from obtaining ratification of the old League of Nations Charter. This U.S. formula, of course, was a compromise, but it was particularly dangerous to the regional organizations. What would you do if you couldn't act even in self-defense? If you couldn't get authorization from the Security Council with the veto power?

"Many say that this United States formula was not satisfactory even for the British and for many Americans. I was quite interested to read in the Yalta papers published by the State Department the following—it is in the notes of Ambassador Bohlen on the February 4th meeting. He wrote this:

> 'In reply to an inquiry of the Prime Minister in regard to the American proposal for solution of the voting question, Mr. Bohlen remarked that the American proposal reminded him of the story of the Southern planter who had given a bottle of whisky to a Negro as a present. The next day he asked the Negro how he had liked the whisky, to which the Negro replied that it was perfect. The planter asked him what he meant. The Negro said if it had been any better it wouldn't have been given to him, and if it had been any worse, he could not have drunk it.'

"And then Mr. Bohlen added this:

> 'Soon thereafter, the Prime Minister and Mr. Eden took their departure, obviously in disagreement with the voting procedure of the Security Council.'

"I don't blame them. Thus, you can understand why, when we

were called to the meeting in San Francisco, we decided to fight this. So we fought in San Francisco against the formula, along the same lines that we had suggested to the United States in 1820, in 1946, and after the war, on the theory that we needed a self-defense pact, period.

"We fought not only for priority of the regional organizations in the settlement of disputes. What we insisted on was the right of self-defense. This right did not exist in the Yalta formula but was embodied in Article 51 of the United Nations Charter.

"We must pay tribute to the American delegates who helped us [obtain the inclusion of Article 51]: Senator Vandenberg, Nelson Rockefeller, and Foster Dulles, who at that time was only the counselor of the American delegation, and to Dr. Albert Lleras of Colombia, who was the leader of the idea and was president of one of the commissions.

"The fight was so difficult that Senator Vandenberg had to send a cable to the President of the United States threatening to resign if the Latin-American self-defense formula was not adopted.

"So what is called the Vandenberg compromise is really a compromise imposed on Secretary Stettinius, along the following lines:

"First, that we would put in Article 51 with its right of self-defense; and second, that we would accept Article 53 (that is the Article which gives the Security Council the power in enforcement actions) but on one condition, namely, that immediately after San Francisco we would have a conference to write the self-defense treaty we had been asking for since 1820. And so we got the commitments, and this is why we had the Rio Conference in 1947.

"Foster Dulles had a very good book that explained the situation and said:

'Thanks to Article 51, we were able to organize a defense within the Charter, but outside of the veto.'

"So it was at the Rio Conference [the Inter-American Treaty of Reciprocal Assistance, Rio de Janeiro, 1947] that the treaty on self-defense, that we had wanted since 1820, was written, and more or less on the same terms suggested by us in 1820." *

---

* See page 13, *supra*.

The Rio Treaty led to the creation of the Organization of American States at Bogotá in 1948.

According to Professor OLIVER, it is "truly unique as an international organization. I think it now safe to say, and subject to challenge and discourse by others here, I now do say, that the Organization of American States is the only 'regional organization' in the sense of Chapter VIII of the Charter of the United Nations. Note that the Organization of American States is not a 'TO' organization, not a NA*TO* or a SEA*TO* or a CEN*TO*. It is not a mere defense treaty organization; it is an *organization of States*. It is not set up primarily as a collective self-defense organization under Article 51 of the Charter. It is set up really as a hemispheric international organization to do jobs outside of the security field as well as within it. Its main function, it seems to me, is very much like that of the United Nations, but junior grade and for the Western Hemisphere.

"I do not know of any other organization that is quite like it. NATO, as we know, is primarily a defense structure in being. Its main objective is defense. It does have vestigial economic, cultural and welfare functions, but they are quite vestigial. As a matter of fact, in the present discourse and discussion about the strengthening of an Atlantic Community or the creation of something over and beyond NATO, undoubtedly some of the functions and some of the organizational structures of the Organization of American States must have suggested themselves to the planners.

"Secondly, hemispheric solidarity, an ideal that underlies the OAS, is an ideal that historically has had long and strong support from our sisters in the Western Hemisphere. It is not unimportant, it seems to me, that it was the Latin-American countries of this hemisphere that insisted at the Chapultepec Conference of 1945, and later at San Francisco, that a larger place be made for the regional organization which came to be called the Organization of American States than had been written into the Dumbarton Oaks Plan for the United Nations.

"The United States, I have a hunch, would, if left to its own devices at that time, have preferred to keep the Western Hemisphere organization relatively less structured than it came out of Chapultepec and San Francisco, and Rio and Bogotá.

"I do not mean to imply that the outlook and ideal of North America towards organization in the Western Hemisphere was negative, not at all. But I think it has been a rather different outlook or ideal than that of the Latin-American countries.

"One of the objectives of the Latin-American countries has been to contain in a legal way by treaty the power and the authority of the United States. The efforts toward organization, going back to the Montevideo Conference of 1933, show quite clearly, I think, that the United States, trying to reassure its neighbors, entered into legal commitments with respect to its use of force . . . the Monroe Doctrine and the like. But the result of what we have done has been to commit us to curb our will as required by a form of international organization that has its own norms, rules, and limitations upon national conduct."

Mr. CHAYES also explained the unique nature of the structure and functions of the OAS: "NATO and SEATO and the Warsaw Pact are organized to exercise collective self-defense, within the term that is referred to in Article 51. But the OAS is much more than a defense organization; it is kind of a junior grade U.N. in the sense that it exercises within its regional sphere all of the kinds of activities that the U.N. engages in, world-wide. It is quite interesting to note that the regional instruments for Latin America of such United Nations agencies as the World Health Organization and UNESCO are all OAS agencies.

"You don't have anything like that in NATO or SEATO or CENTO, or the Warsaw Pact. They are defensive organizations, almost pure and simple, whereas the OAS is a structure designed to deal on a broad scale with the problems of international living in the hemisphere. It is designed to regulate disputes within the hemisphere when they become threats to the peace. And I think it is in that sense that all of us—the Ambassador, Professor Oliver, and I—see a unique character to the OAS, which does not occur in the other collective defense organizations.

"What we said was that this was the conception of a regional organization that is in Chapter VIII of the U.N. Charter; not in Article 51 but in Chapter VIII, which deals with regional organizations. If you look at Chapter VIII as a whole, most of its provisions do not have any relevance to an organization like NATO or SEATO, but all of its provisions have relevance and meaning when seen in the framework of an organization like the OAS."

Ambassador URRUTIA agreed with the views of Professor Oliver and Mr. Chayes, but emphasized the need to remember the main purpose of the OAS: "Definitely, I think that the Organization of American States is the only regional organization to fit within Chapter VIII of the Charter. But may I say, too, that sometimes Ambassadors in Washington have the impression that, because we have many other joint activities under Chapter VIII, we can forget the main purpose of the OAS. It is only now that the self-defense purpose is being stressed. For many, many years, we were only invited to numerous cocktails in Washington for artistic organizations, art, culture, anything, but nothing about self-defense. We say, yes, Chapter VIII of the Charter is very important because many activities must be considered. First of all, economic ones are very important, but the main one is self-defense. Let's not forget that this is the main purpose of the organization."

C. *The Cuban Quarantine: Collective Action or Unilateral United States Policy?*

"Too often", said Mr. CHAYES, "discussion of the quarantine, even professional discussion, has proceeded as though it was a unilateral exercise of force by the United States directed against the Soviet Union.

"That is understandable, of course. The threat was a Soviet threat; it was met largely by the power and will of the United States. It was President Kennedy who first alerted the world to the presence of offensive weapons on Cuban soil. Of course without the U.S. Navy and Armed Forces in reserve, the quarantine would have been an empty gesture.

"Legal analysis, however, must get behind the headline writer's view of the events of the past few weeks. When it does, I think we will see that in very important ways those events reflect and are the product of hemispheric institutions that Professor Oliver has described in his Working Paper. For the presence of nuclear weapons in Cuba was a threat not only to ourselves, but also to the entire hemisphere, and the action taken to meet it was not unilateral. It was taken in concert with the other nations of the hemisphere.

"As you know, the quarantine was not proclaimed until after

the Organ of Consultation of the OAS had passed its resolutions under Articles 6 and 8 of the Rio Treaty."*

Professor OLIVER, in his comments, interjected the question of whether or not the United States considered the OAS as merely a rubber stamp "clearance" for United States policy in the Cuban crisis:

"The attitude of the United States towards what is now the Organization of American States has been one mainly of getting what in government one would call 'clearance' for action by us. We have not asked the Organization of American States, we have not asked our sister republics in World War II, or later, to take action along with us. We have really asked them to permit us to act without objection by them.

"In World War II, as history records, and as I mention in this paper, for reasons of military housekeeping, our Armed Forces, at least our decision makers in the Armed Forces, were reluctant to accept the proffers of explicit cooperation made by a number of Latin American countries. The service of supply and training problems were just too complicated. Also, when it came to lend-lease and military assistance, our military people preferred to work on a bilateral basis, rather than on a multilateral basis.

"It should not escape our attention whether the attitude I have just described as an historic one may not have its counterpart in developments that have taken place so far in the current Cuban crisis.

"I have read in the papers that several of the Latin-American states have offered assistance, naval units, and the like, but I have seen nothing indicating that that assistance has been accepted.

"I mention this, not argumentatively or critically, but simply to try to show what I believe to be somewhat different objectives as between the Latin-American states and ourselves with respect to the legal organization of the hemisphere."

Mr. NUNEZ responded:

"I would like to comment on Professor Oliver's statement concerning the assistance which has been offered from Latin America during the current crisis. I think it is a fact that there are two vessels today of the Argentine Navy patrolling the waters off

---

* See page 26, *supra.*

Cuba, and that there are air crews of the Argentine Air Force participating in such a venture, and there is one brigade of troops in Argentina which is ready to sail for the Caribbean at any moment if the international security organization known as the OAS wishes it to act.

"I think that that is only an isolated instance. There are other units which have been offered and have been incorporated. So that as the crisis develops, there will be available active participants in the form of individuals willing to risk their lives in the common struggle."

Mr. CHAYES then added the following information on the collective nature of the OAS action:

"The action was concerted action. We have already heard Professor Oliver doubt that other nations of the hemisphere have contributed, and Mr. Nunez allayed the doubt. The fact is that eleven nations of the hemisphere have contributed either vessels, troops, or facilities to the operation of the quarantine, and there is now a joint quarantine command operating under Admiral Dennison.

"When I talk of the collective character of the action that we have taken in the Cuban crisis, I often get this reply from people: 'What if the OAS had not responded? Would the United States have gone ahead on its own in that case?'

"And I say that to ask that question is like asking what would have happened if Congress had not declared war on December 8, 1941. In the circumstances, it was just not conceivable that the OAS would not respond.

"Once the proof of the reality of the threat from Cuba was certain, the response from the inter-American system was also certain. The President acted on the assumption that the inter-American system would operate as it was intended to operate. I think he took a certain risk in so acting. But, certainly, one of the gains from the crisis is the knowledge that that assumption—that the inter-American system would operate as it was intended to operate—was justified."

D. *Interpretations of the OAS Resolution*

What action did the OAS authorize in the Cuban crisis?*

---

* See page 27, *supra.*

Mr. NUNEZ felt that "as a practical matter, in the present crisis, it is clear that the United States and the OAS will have almost complete liberty of action in dealing with the Cuban issue. I think that Dr. Mora of the OAS has stated that even armed invasion by United States troops would not be in any way a violation of the OAS resolution."

Mr. CHAYES explained in detail the action authorized by the OAS resolution:

". . . some question has been raised tonight about the scope of that resolution and what in form it authorizes, and I think those who have said that it is a very far-reaching resolution indeed are right.

"The operative paragraph recommends that member States take all measures individually and collectively, including the use of armed force, which they may deem necessary to insure that the Government of Cuba cannot continue to receive from the Sino-Soviet powers military materiel and related supplies which threaten the peace and security of the continent. That is the first half and the second half is: 'and to prevent the missiles in Cuba with offensive capability from ever becoming an active threat to the peace and security of the continent.'

"One of the speakers mentioned that Secretary Mora of the OAS had given a very broad interpretation to that paragraph.

"I think we have even more interesting evidence of the scope of the paragraph in the legislative history of its adoption. The one element of dissent in that whole meeting of the OAS on October 23rd, 1962, was that Brazil, Mexico and Bolivia abstained on the portion of the second part of the operative paragraph of the resolution which recommends member States take measures to 'prevent the missiles in Cuba with offensive capability from ever becoming an active threat to the peace and security of the continent.'

"The Brazilian delegate abstained because he said he thought this language authorized an invasion of Cuba, whereas all that was needed to authorize the quarantine was the first part of that paragraph.

"Now, with that comment from the Brazilian delegate and that interpretation of the article placed on it by the Brazilian delegate, no one disagreed. No one argued with him on that point. The other delegates voted for that clause with that interpretation placed on it. When we consider the scope of the resolution as it was intended by the OAS Organ of Consultation, that is a very important feature to remember."

A member of the audience raised the issue of the legality of the reconnaissance flights over Cuba, the authority for them, and particularly the question of fighting off attacks on such flights. Professor OLIVER felt the problem was a difficult one.

"It is awfully hard with the best will in the world to say that a state that shoots at hostile aircraft over its territory is engaging in aggression. That particular part is very difficult to say. I am speaking of the Cuban use of force against our aircraft.

"But what is much more difficult to say is that intervention to protect the aircraft that are being shot at is not an illegal use of force. It is a very difficult question, indeed.

"Now we have taken our position. I take it that we are going to defend the aircraft against anti-aircraft action in Cuba. Will that lead to bombing interdiction of anti-aircraft sites? After all, there are a number of different operations, as any old airman knows, that have to be engaged in when you receive flack from the ground. There is not only evasive action; there is convoy by fighter aircraft; there is interdiction of the anti-aircraft batteries on the ground. And when you get to that third phase, all I can say is that you have, even under the present arrangements, a most difficult problem indeed.

"I should hope that we could keep our aircraft at a reconnaissance level and quite high."

Mr. CHAYES did not find the problem so difficult and, in fact, thought that the OAS resolution contained the answer to the problem:

"I don't think it is fair to leave the impression that the issue of what can or should be done in defense of the aircraft is properly framed by asking whether, if Cuban anti-aircraft, assuming they are Cuban, fire on our planes, that can be characterized as aggression. There would be a simpler line of analysis as long as we are talking about the legalities of the problem, and that is that the OAS resolution covers reconnaissance flights, and validates those activities. We then must be entitled to take what defensive measures are necessary in order to conduct those flights, and that seems to me to be fairly within the legal ambit of the OAS resolution.

"That is the line of analysis which I think is indicated legally

42

rather than asking whether the Cubans have committed aggression by firing on the planes. If the activity is itself validated by the OAS resolution, and I think everybody here has said that it is, then you can't say that you have to send those fliers over defenseless. You just can't say that. The validation of the activity includes validation of necessary measures to defend them."

Professor OLIVER then elaborated the difficulty in justifying action to defend reconnaissance flights from attack:

"As to the aggression, I want to explain the point. What I am trying to get at is this: if you can't call Cuba's firing aggression—but what? self-defense, anticipatory, or otherwise?—then it makes the countermeasures in defense of aircraft taken by us the more difficult to justify. That is what I was trying to explain.

"As far as I, as a newspaper reader, am concerned, I have read statements that our air people say they are 'to protect our own'. I hope the problem develops just as Mr. Chayes describes it. I think that is the way it should be: 'Collective action reconnaissance.' But what I have read as a newspaper reader is that the Air Force says it will protect its own, and I think that is a little bit different."

Mr. NUNEZ was asked whether the OAS resolution endorsing the United States initiative in the Cuban situation reflected only the view of the conservative forces in Latin America on the Cuban revolution and on Cuba's alliance with Russia. Mr. NUNEZ replied:

"The answer to that question is that the Latin American action from a purely juridical standpoint has occurred through the voice of their established governments. Now, if we want to analyze here tonight whether those governments represent the conservative body of opinion in these countries or socialist-oriented groups which are favorable to Mr. Castro, I think many of you will miss your train.

"There has been in this country a fundamental misconception concerning the strength of Mr. Castro and his appeal to the so-called socialist-oriented groups in these countries.

"In my judgment, the governments and peoples of Latin America have been looking at Mr. Castro and what he represents with a great deal of concern and worry for a considerable period of time. The sigh that came up from Latin America when Mr. Kennedy gave his speech must have been almost audible here in New York. I think that you can make no distinction funda-

43

mentally between the so-called conservative elements in these countries and the socialist-oriented.

"Basically, the majority of the people in Latin America see in Mr. Castro a fundamental threat to their way of life and to their freedom, and they will react accordingly. As Mr. Chayes has pointed out, their reaction has been clear and unmistaken."

II. WAS THE CUBAN QUARANTINE LEGAL UNDER THE UNITED NATIONS CHARTER?

A. *Was it Self-Defense under Article 51 or a Violation of Article 53?*

Article 51 of the Charter provides:

> "Nothing in the present Charter shall impair the inherent right of individual or collective self-defense if an armed attack occurs against a Member of the United Nations, until the Security Council has taken the measures necessary to maintain international peace and security . . ."

Article 53 (1) of the Charter states in part:

> "The Security Council shall, where appropriate, utilize such regional arrangements or agencies for enforcement action under its authority. But no enforcement action shall be taken under regional arrangements or by regional agencies without the authorization of the Security Council . . ."

Article 53 means to some observers that before any action was taken to meet the Soviet threat in Cuba, the OAS or the United States or both, should have gone to the Security Council for authorization.

Ambassador URRUTIA felt the Cuba crisis confirmed his view of a conflict between Articles 51 and 53 of the Charter:

"The problem is that all we got in San Francisco was Article 51. We were not able to get more than that. According to Article 51, we can only act in self-defense in case of armed attacks. Enforcement action can only be authorized by the Security Council.

"International lawyers for many years have been discussing what is the difference between self-defense and enforcement action, and it is not very easy. The Vandenberg compromise was only in Article 51, and the great powers put in Article 53 which, unfortunately, contains this sentence: 'But no enforcement action shall be taken under regional arrangements or by regional agencies without authorization of the Security Council.' So technically, according to Article 53, we ought to wait for an authorization of the Security Council, if we want to take enforcement actions. That is the result if you interpret Article 53 literally.

"Many of us, even before the Cuban crisis, had the idea that if there were a conflict between Article 51 and Article 53, Article 51 must prevail. Our argument is that Article 51 says: 'Nothing in the present Charter shall impair the inherent right of individual or collective self-defense . . .'

"A conflict of interpretation may exist between Article 51 and Article 53 but as, on the one hand, Article 53 gives exclusively to the Security Council the authority to order enforcement action and, on the other hand, Article 51 authorizes the use of force in self-defense, I think that our inherent right of self-defense is at stake in the Cuban crisis and must prevail.

"We must face the facts. We have difficulty; and the lawyers will find difficulty between Article 51 and Article 53. But I think it is much better to face it, to see that the difficulty exists, and to very frankly go back to what we have claimed since 1820: that self-defense is a primary objective for our countries, and that this regional organization is important, and a self-defense pact first of all. If there is a conflict between Article 51 and Article 53, the Latin-American states will take 51."

Mr. CHAYES, however, felt that in the circumstances of the Cuban crisis these Articles are reconcilable. He pointed out that neither President Kennedy in his speech nor the OAS resolution invoked Article 51. Mr. CHAYES described the quarantine as the kind of action by regional organizations to keep the peace envisaged in Chapter VIII of the Charter and contemplated by Article 52 (1) of the Charter which prescribes the use of "regional arrangements or agencies for dealing with such matters relating to the maintenance of national peace and security as are appropriate for regional action." He said:

"I agree with Ambassador Urrutia that the framers of the Charter intended that the Security Council would exercise the broadest powers over disputes or situations which threatened or breached the peace. As originally conceived, it was the Security Council that was to act as policeman for maintaining order and preventing the disruption of peace. But I don't find the problem of reconciling Article 51 and Article 53 as difficult as the Ambassador does, because the practice of the United Nations as a living institution has not wholly confirmed the conceptions of the draftsmen. And we, who practice the common law and live under a constitutional system, know that institutional practice is as important and often more important for the operation of law than is original intention.

"In this light, I am not at all sure that Professor Oliver's three propositions state the whole of the relation between the U.N. and regional organizations in the field of peacekeeping.*

"As we all know, the Security Council has been at least partially paralyzed by the veto. Other agencies have necessarily moved in to fill the void created by this paralysis.

"The most familiar instance of this process is the General Assembly's assertion of jurisdiction to deal with peacekeeping problems, as, for example, in the latter stages of the Korean War and in the Suez crisis.

"The Secretary-General has also assumed a significant role, a significantly independent role and one that was not originally anticipated. And we see that in the Congo dispute and, indeed, in the development of the Cuban crisis in the last couple of weeks.

"A regional organization like the OAS is another obvious candidate for the peacekeeping role within its regional terms of reference.

"These developments in practical U.N. politics—the shrinkage of the Security Council and the expansion of the role of other agencies—have had to be reconciled with the language of the Charter.

"This is a familiar process, for the Charter is a constitutional document, and all of us know that only experience can give precision to its terms. In this case, experience has worked to refine the concept of 'enforcement action.'

"I put that in quotes because it turns out to be a technical term, and not a popular term, in the light of the experience of the U.N. The result of the experience has been to give this concept of enforcement action a very narrow scope. In recent months, last summer, in fact, in its opinion on U.N. finances [I. C. J. Advisory Opinion of July 20, 1962, on Certain Expenses of the United Nations], the International Court of Justice confirmed the shift of peacekeeping responsibility to the General Assembly. In that case it held that the Congo and Middle East operations were not

---

* See page 11, *supra.*

enforcement actions, even though they involved the use of force to meet threats to the peace. They were not enforcement actions because the measures taken were not obligatory on the members.

"On the other hand, earlier in the Security Council—this is back in 1958—in dealing with the sanctions against the Dominican Republic, and last spring in dealing with the Punta del Este measures taken against Cuba, the Security Council refused to treat diplomatic or economic sanctions by the OAS as enforcement action.

"If you put these two lines of precedent together, you will see what a narrow ambit a decade and a half of international history has left for the concept of 'enforcement action' [under Article 53]."

B. *Was the Soviet Action in Cuba an "armed attack" within the Meaning of Article 51?*

The problem remains as to the applicability to the Cuban crisis of the right of self-defense embodied in Article 51 of the United Nations Charter.

Article 51 guarantees the inherent right of individual or collective self-defense if an *armed attack* occurs against a member of the United Nations. Does Article 51 permit self-defense only if an armed attack occurs or, also, if a member of the United Nations believes itself threatened?

Mr. NUNEZ indicated the flexibility of the concept of "armed attack": "It need not be an attack, for example, of armed forces of a non-continental or foreign power. An armed insurrection from within aided from abroad would certainly fit into that definition and could become the foundation for action. Professor Berle in his recent book reported a very interesting excerpt of testimony before the Senate Foreign Relations Committee, when it considered the NATO Treaty, where Secretary Acheson addressed himself particularly to this phrase, 'armed attack,' as it applied within the concept of the NATO Treaty."

Ambassador URRUTIA advocated a practical definition of armed attack "because, in the atomic age, a country cannot wait for a missile to be fired to start its self-defense—when a missile is fired it is too late to take defensive action. An armed attack in an atomic age starts when you start building bases and putting missiles a few miles from the continent."

48

III. THE CUBAN CRISIS AS PRECEDENT

A. *The Cuban Crisis as Precedent in the Development of the Inter-American Security System*

Professor TANNENBAUM described the long-range effect of the crisis on hemispheric solidarity:

"So far as our relations with Latin America are concerned, and in some ways our relations with the rest of the world, but certainly so far as our relations with Latin America are concerned, they will never be the same again.

"This confrontation of Russia on the Cuban issue has set up, and I think set up permanently, the inescapable fact that, politically speaking, the Western Hemisphere is a unity. And this is very important.

"I am talking as a historian; you are all talking as lawyers. As a historian now, looking at what has happened, you have unanimous approval by the nations of a continent-and-a-half of an action taken by the United States in a time of crisis, which, for all practical purposes, makes this hemisphere politically, in times of crises, a united entity.

"That does not mean that our problems with Latin America will not continue now, and that all of our difficulties will be resolved. Put somehow the relationship between ourselves and Latin America has been given a different tone. It has been given a different 'ambiente,' a different environment.

"Latin Americans now realize, as they never did before—perhaps we do, too—that for good or ill, and for all times to come, we are in the same boat vis-a-vis the rest of the world.

"There has been some question about this in the past, both among ourselves and among our Latin-American friends, and certainly among outsiders. That question has been answered. If I had the time, and you had the patience, I could go into a fairly long historical statement of how this came about. I could argue, and I hope convincingly, that there is something of a common experience in this hemisphere which belongs to the people of this hemisphere, and which is unique among themselves; and which, in time of real crisis—when the chips are down—manifested itself as it has.

"I would suggest that this both makes it easier for us and for the Latin Americans to face the problems of the future and in some ways makes it more difficult.

"I would also suggest that what has happened vis-a-vis Cuba, makes the Alliance for Progress a more meaningful undertaking, and gives it a different kind of urgency and significance. Whether it is a success or failure is another matter.

"It establishes a basis for a responsible relationship between ourselves and Latin America of a type that some of us perhaps were not prepared to agree to in the past."

Mr. NUNEZ commented on Professor Tannenbaum's observations:

Fundamentally and most importantly the Cuban crisis has clearly established that the inter-American security system, supplied with leadership, is perfectly capable of facing the modern techniques of Communist subversion and aggression.

"The abstract and broad concepts spelled out in the Rio Treaty and the Bogota Charter have proven to have sufficient flexibility to claim the allegiance of the United States in a moment of grave crisis.

"It can only be hoped that this fact will give us greater confidence in using this mechanism and in leading the system along the path that is essential to the security of the free world.

"Professor Tannenbaum has said that he feels that this present crisis has clearly indicated to the Latin Americans that we are all in the same boat.

"I would suggest that Latin Americans have known for a long time that they have been in the same boat. The only question has been who is pulling the oar. In this crisis the United States has clearly shown not only its willingness, but its capability, of grasping the oar and taking the boat where it has to go. And Latin America has proven that it will accept such leadership, and will eagerly follow it.

"The international security institution, known as the OAS, has established legal and juridical concepts within which contemporary political leadership can act and function. This has been its aim, and in my judgment it has been successful. Any attempt to derive from the Rio Treaty or the Bogota Charter specific constants of

50

policy is a grave error which must be avoided and which, unfortunately, many of us as lawyers are only too prone to do. We cannot find in these instruments the answers to specific foreign policy problems.

"What the system has proven is that its creators had a particular kind of foresight in creating an elastic institution in which developing economic and political concepts can live."

Professor OLIVER singled out one of the major problems to be faced by the OAS, namely, its role in dealing with revolutions in member countries:

"We are going to have the very serious problem of distinguishing the made-in-Moscow revolution from the indigenous social upheaval in various countries. And that is especially difficult because in many of these countries the upheaval is going to be sparked by leftist elements, some of which are under the general ideological influence of Moscow. Some are lackeys of Moscow but most of them are the indigenous revolutionaries in these countries.

"Cuba is an example of a political and social revolution that went bad. In a way, Cuba was a very telescoped version of the Mexican Revolution. At least it started in political action against a dictator, as Madero versus Diaz, but in a very short period of time it evolved into a social revolution as well, and the social revolution was traduced."

Professor OLIVER stressed that neither the United States nor the OAS had used their regional authority to destroy a disliked revolutionary government, but had acted in self-defense leaving the ultimate resolution of the Cuban social revolution to forces within the country.

"The long-range objective has been the demise of the Castro regime in Cuba, but our policy in this crisis has left that demise to the operation of ordinary political and economic forces in that country."

B. *The Cuban Crisis as Precedent in the Development of International Law*

The Forum participants were asked, "How would you state in international legal terms the rule of law for which the Cuban case stands?"

Professor OLIVER replied "that the Cuban crisis so far stands

51

juridically for an expansion of the idea of self-defense beyond response to overt aggression, and into the realm of anticipatory self-defense. The position taken so far is that it is all right under the Charter of the U.N., and under the Charter of the OAS to take collective measures in anticipation of a clear missile or related technological threat, and that such action, to the extent taken so far, is legal; legal in the sense that there has been no legal objection to it. The care with which the proposals were formulated and acted upon reflected a measure of self-restraint in the exercise of what I now call anticipatory self-defense.

"The notion of anticipatory self-defense is one that should be handled with great care, obviously. It is no doctrine for the quick-trigger boys. Anticipatory self-defense in the international community is not unlike the common law doctrine of self-defense in my native Texas. In most states you have to retreat to the wall. In Texas, when he may be reaching for his handkerchief, and you think it is a gun, you can beat him to the draw.

"That is about the situation that we are in now. At the present time, we have been careful. But this doctrine of anticipatory self-defense has as its outer limit prevention of war or aggression, and the problem is where you draw the line. And that is exactly what I referred to in the question of 'what next' in Cuba.

"The point is we have a new dimension for self-defense, and one that is law already, because we got away with it. I mean that seriously, don't take me as a cynic at this point. If you are careful, as the legal adviser has stated, in the direction you give to evolution, we common law lawyers expect that the law will grow and develop to meet new needs, such as this atomic missile threat in Cuba. But the law grows and develops by increments, and that is what we have seen so far in Cuba."

Ambassador URRUTIA added this observation:

"I think anticipatory collective self-defense would be the word; and second, when you say that that is legal because it has not been contested, I agree one hundred per cent. And I would like to add it has not been contested even by the Soviet. So that from now on in these interpretations of Articles 51 and 53, we have a precedent, and that is that anticipatory self-defense was not contested by the Soviet Union.

"The Organization of American States had made recommendations in Guatemala in 1954, then Santo Domingo, Costa Rica,

52

Punta del Este. On the Guatemala action, the Soviets objected. When the Santo Domingo revolution occurred, the Soviets again insisted on the approval of the Security Council. On the Costa Rica action and the Punta del Este action, they objected and said it was illegal because the Security Council had not authorized them.

"For the first time, in the Cuba case, when we went much further, the Soviets did not object. So this is the first time that the Soviet Union has not taken the position that those actions could not be taken by the regional organizations without the authorization of the Security Council. In that way it is a legal precedent."

C. The Cuban Crisis as Precedent in the Development of International Relations

Professor TANNENBAUM suggested: ". . . that the confrontation of Russia over Cuba, has had—both morally and politically from the point of view of broad, basic international relations and the structure of international power—a very wholesome impact, not only on Latin America but also on the rest of the world and especially upon Russia, I should hope.

"I am not much of an optimist; but if one assumes that many nations are capable of learning from experience . . . one would have to assume that as a result of this experience over Cuba, the Russians and perhaps other nations in the world have been brought back to a certain sense of realism about the nature and the character of the present world situation.

"I would say . . . that Russia had been behaving in the world in recent years as if she were living in a vacuum, as if she were free to move in any direction and make threats about doing this and doing that, whenever she had a mind to, without reason or with reason.

"I would hope that what has happened in the last few weeks will have brought a certain amount of realism into international relations and a certain sense of the limitations within which nations great and small operate in this world.

"I would like to suggest to you that what has happened over Cuba has revealed something, like a sudden flash of lightning, which some of us perhaps very dimly perceived, but which should become evident, and which shows up the nature of the world situation, for good or for ill.

53

"If you assume that man is not destined to commit suicide . . . the Cuban crisis has revealed that neither of the great powers, Russia nor the United States, has freedom of movement; Russia cannot move into Cuba, for the same reason that we cannot move into Hong Kong, or that we could not let France and England move into Egypt. Something has happened to the very structure of international relations; the great powers of the world are powerless; they can't move, really."

Mr. CHAYES noted the restraints on regional organizations themselves:

"Regional organizations, of course, remain subject to check even where, as in this case, they employ agreed procedures and processes. They are subordinate to the U.N. by the terms of the Charter, and in the case of the OAS, by the terms of the relevant inter-American treaties themselves. Like an individual state, a regional organization can be called to account for its action in the appropriate agency of the parent organization.

"In recognition of this relationship the President ordered that the case be put immediately before the Security Council. The U.N. through the Council and the Secretary-General is as of this moment actively engaged in the effort to develop a permanent solution to the threats to peace represented by the Soviet nuclear capability in Cuba."

Taken together with other recent peacekeeping actions, Mr. CHAYES saw in the Cuban quarantine another significance:

"Since World War II, each of the actions to keep the peace in Korea, in the Middle East, in the Congo, in Lebanon, and now in Cuba has taken a different operational form. But each of them reflects our conviction that a breach of the peace involves us all, and that we must meet it together through the institutions of collective security established for that purpose.

"The quarantine seen in this framework is, I think, a significant contribution to the developing body of post-war experience with collective responsibility and collective action to preserve the peace."

IV. THE ROLE OF THE LAWYER AND THE LAW IN THE CUBAN CRISIS

A. *The Role of the Lawyer*

Professor OLIVER emphasized that the Cuban crisis ". . . has been a real triumph for the lawyer and his role in decision-making. . . . The lawyer in this crisis has not been a mere nay-sayer. It is perfectly obvious to anyone who knows anything about the legal issues involved that they were carefully considered and that plans were made in this crisis with the legal situation in mind. This I sense, because far too often in my own government experience, and I daresay in the wider experience of many others of you, we have let the activist, the impatient patriot, the 'damn the torpedoes' and 'Let the bombs fall where they may' schools ride roughshod over our interest in a credible international order.

"In history, especially in our historical relationship to peoples that seem to live so constantly and so closely with history as the Latin Americans, the way you do a deed is very important. And I am happy we did it the way we did this time. I am even grateful, speaking of that remarkable description of how government works in the *New York Times* for Saturday, November 2nd—I am very grateful that one of our Russian experts, Llewellyn Thompson, pointed out early in the game how important it was to keep the legal issues in mind, because, as is well known, the Soviets are oriented toward legal niceties.

"This is true. My wife and I knew this as third-row people on an American delegation as early as 1946. I do not understand why the latter-day Machiavellis of the power politics school of American foreign relations have never understood this obvious fact: that law is, as used instrumentally, an important variable in the power process, and, if used intelligently by a master, can achieve sound and desirable foreign policy results, I would say in nine cases out of ten. I only hope that as the crisis continues, this same frame of mind, this same attitude toward the legal issues involved in this crisis will continue."

55

Mr. CHAYES, drawing on his immediate experience in the Cuban crisis as the Legal Adviser to the Departament of State, remarked that he wanted ". . . to thank Professor Oliver for another part of his oral remarks. That was his recognition that the lawyer had a real role in the development of our policy in these last weeks. I can say this without departing from the canons of modesty, because when the beginning of the crisis came, I was in Paris, and the acting legal advisor was another lawyer well-known to many of you, Leonard Meeker. He was called in by the Secretary of State, I think, on Thursday. The *New York Times* gives the impression, which has had some currency added to it tonight, that the reason he was called in was that we thought the Russians might be sensitive to the legalities of the situation. It is true that Ambassador Thompson pointed that out.

"It is also true that from the outset the Secretary of State, the President, and the Attorney General were extraordinarily aware of the relation of our legal position and of the legal elements in the decision to the success of any action that could be taken."

B. *The Role of the Law*

Mr. CHAYES warned that "[o]ne of the pitfalls into which international lawyers are prone to fall is to seek for a norm that says this is legal or it is not legal, in terms of a substantive norm.

"That was reflected in one of the questions tonight. In fact, however, most of us who have had any experience with the American system, and particularly with the public law system— and, after all, international law is a branch in this sense of public law, not of private law—know that the institutional components, the operation of institutions, institutional procedures and processes, are as important in the development of law as the elaboration of substantive norms.

"This case is a perfect example of the interaction among the institutional procedures which validate a particular kind of action, because the institution responds to the particular circumstances. One of the circumstances was that the Soviet Union was over-extended and was in our bailiwick. Whether the institutional response would be the same in a different situation is a different question."

Chairman TONDEL remarked that many were uncomfortably aware of "what the situation would have been if there had been no legal institution to respond to the crisis."

Appendix A

CHRONOLOGICAL OUTLINE

I. The Evolution of the Inter-American System.

   A. From the Latin-American Revolutions (1810-20) through the Roosevelt Corollary.

      1. The inter-American system during this period: largely a cultural association; imbalance of power.

      2. United States and Latin-American national interests, respectively, under the Monroe Doctrine.

      3. No law against unilateral use of national force, until, at the earliest, 1919.

      4. The Roosevelt Corollary to the Monroe Doctrine and United States intervention, 1905-1934.

   B. International undertakings from Montevideo (1933) to Chapultepec (1945).

      1. The Good Neighbor Policy and the juridical commitments at the Montevideo Conference: Latin-American political objectives vis-a-vis the United States cast as law:

        Article IV: [juridical equality of states]

        Article VI: [reducing the legal significance of recognition]

        Article VIII: "No state has the right to intervene in the internal or external affairs of another."

        Article IX: [Foreigners may not claim rights other or more extensive than those of nationals.]

        Article XI: [Agreement not to recognize territorial changes or other advantages obtained by coercive measures; declaration of inviolability of state territory as against occupation or any other imposed measures of force.]

      2. Buenos Aires Conference, December 1-23, 1936: United States and Brazilian proposals for a continuous consultative organization on regional security, including extra-hemispheric threats, was watered down to the *obligation to consult.*

3. Lima, December 9-27, 1938: U. S. proposed organizing in anticipation of trouble in Europe; Argentina, Chile, and Mexico led the Latins to the view that the United States was crying "wolf." Nothing significant as to the creation of a security system was accomplished.

4. Panama, September 23-October 3, 1939: the first meeting of Consultation of the Ministers of Foreign Affairs. Results: (i) the Declaration of Panama proclaiming a wartime neutrality zone of 300 miles around the Americas, enforcement to be provided by national naval units; (ii) ministers to consult should any danger arise that territories held in the Americas by non-American states might be transferred to other such states [a first step toward Latin-American participation in the Monroe Doctrine].

5. Havana, July 21-30, 1940: Resolution XV, the first inter-American security instrument specifically directed against outsiders:

> ". . . any attempt on the part of a non-American state against the integrity or inviolability of the territory, the sovereignty or political independence of an American state shall be considered as an act of aggression against the states which sign this declaration."

Also, the Inter-American Peace Committee was established.

6. The War Years: the Latin-American Staff Agreements; and the January 15-28, 1942 Rio meeting. The latter created the Inter-American Defense Board and recommended the breaking of relations with the Axis Powers.

C. The United Nations and the Inter-American system.
   1. Two views of the world organization: universal with regional auxiliaries; a series of regional arrangements with a central consultative mechanism.

   2. The Latin-American states reacted negatively to the Dumbarton Oaks draft's provision that regional agencies should be entirely subordinate to the authority of the Security Council. Cf. Article 53 of the UN Charter.

   3. Chapultepec, February 21-March 8, 1945. Significant results:
      a. The Latin-American states recommended a greater role for regional organizations in the United Nations; and

      b. Called for a treaty to continue Havana Resolution XV into the postwar and for continued consultation on collective measures against aggression.

4. The problem at the San Francisco Conference, April, 1945, and Senator Vandenberg's formula for resolving the problem. Cf. Article 51 of the United Nations Charter. Contrast Article 53, the original Dumbarton Oaks proposal. *Question*: under the Charter, how free is a regional arrangement to make decisions as to the use of force: (i) Against aggression? (ii) To deal with threats or breaches of the peace within the regional system? (iii) In collective self-defense?

II. The Organization of American States Etablished: Legal Aspects.

A. The Inter-American Treaty of Reciprocal Assistance, Rio de Janeiro, 1947. Main features:

1. Covers aggression from any source.

2. Armed attack against any American state within the hemisphere gives rise automatically to an obligation on states individually to assist the victim.

3. Provides for consultation as to aggressions that are not armed attacks.

4. Does not provide a structure-in-being for defense.

5. Voting formula for the organs of consultation: 2/3 rather than unanimity; no veto.

6. Inter-American security system is carefully fitted into the United Nations Charter by (i) declaring its functions to be defensive and (ii) stipulation that no provision of the Rio Treaty shall be construed so as to conflict with the Charter of the U.N.

B. The Charter of the Organization of American States, Bogotá, 1948.

1. The civics of the Organization, mainly in reference to its continuous representative body (Council) and its Secretariat (Pan American Union). Contrasts as to organizational features with the UN and with NATO.

2. The "Principles" and the Duty not to Intervene:

Article 5. (d) ". . . effective representative democracy".

Article 15. "No state or group of states has the right to intervene, directly or indirectly, for any reason whatever, in the internal or external affairs of any other state. The foregoing principle prohibits not only armed force but also any other form of interference or attempted threat against the personality of the State or against its political, economic, and cultural elements." [Reflections on this "ultimate" in prohibition of intervention, in relationship to the present crisis. Is UN intervention also proscribed?]

Article 16. "No state may use or encourage the use of coercive measures of an economic or political character in order to force the sovereign will of another State and obtain from it advantages of any kind."

[Further reflections as to Cuba in regard to cutting the sugar quota, choking off trade with Cuba. Are collective economic sanctions barred, as collective armed intervention is under Article 15?]

III. The Established Inter-American System and the Threat of Sino-Soviet Intrusion.

A. The Caracas Declaration, 1954.

1. Secretary Dulles' strongest support, in a generally apathetic atmosphere, came from Cuba, the Dominican Republic, Peru, Nicaragua, El Salvador, and Venezuela, *all under dictatorships.*

2. Mr. Dulles invoked the Monroe Doctrine as opposed to international communism and characterized it as multilateral:
". . . These sentiments have long ceased to be unilateral. They have become the accepted principle of this hemisphere. That is why it seems to us we would be false to our past unless we again proclaimed that the extension to this hemisphere of alien despotism would be a danger to us all, which we unitedly oppose."

3. The Declaration:
". . . [T]he domination or control of the political institutions of an American state by the international Communist movement, extending to this Hemisphere the political system of an extra-continental power, would constitute a threat to the sovereignty and independence of the American states, endangering the peace of America and would call for a meeting of consultation to consider the adoption of measures in accordance with existing treaties. . . . This declaration of foreign policy made by the American Republics in relation to dangers originating outside this Hemisphere is designed to protect and not

to impair the inalienable right of each American state
freely to choose its own form of government and economic
system and to live its own social and cultural life."

4. Did the Caracas Declaration "Pan Americanize" the
   Monroe Doctrine? An analysis:

   a. The statement of an expert [Mecham]: ". . . Thus by
      action of the Caracas conference the principles of the
      Monroe Doctrine became the common policy of the
      American Republics. The Pan Americanization of the
      famous policy of President Monroe was now accom-
      plished."

   b. Does "Pan Americanization" equal "no longer capable
      of unilateral application"?

   c. Did abandonment of the Roosevelt Corollary at Mon-
      tevideo (1933) and at Bogota (1948) bar all possible
      unilateral use of force? What about multilateral inter-
      vention under the Caracas Declaration? What about
      multilateral consent to unilateral use of force against
      alien political subversion?

   d. To what extent, after the UN Charter, could the
      United States, without reference to the inter-American
      system, have used force unilaterally to assert its na-
      tional interest as expressed in the Monroe Doctrine?
      Is unilateral intervention to throw out a Communist
      regime "self defense" under the Charter?

   e. To what extent do the answers in *d* change if collective
      action by the OAS states is taken?

   f. What if a Western Hemisphere country really does, as a
      matter of its initiative and free will, invite a Com-
      munist power in?

B. Juridical Aspects of the Guatemalan Crisis of 1954.
   1. Guatemala referred its charge of invasion from Honduras
      to both the Security Council and the Inter-American
      Peace Committee, then later attempted to withdraw the
      latter reference.

   2. The debate at the Security Council.

      a. Issue: should the Security Council withold action
         where aggression was charged pending fact-finding
         and consideration by the regional arrangement?

      b. Guatemalan legal position: no "dispute" with Hondu-
         ras; the "situation" is one of aggression: the Security

63

Council should act. The Soviet representative vigorously agreed.

c. The Lodge-Tsarapkin verbal duel; a sample from the
Official Record:

". . . The United States representative asked
with emotion what was the reason for the Soviet
Union's present attitude . . . why was it interesting itself in the Western Hemisphere. He even
voiced the suggestion that the Soviet Union had
certain intentions in the Western Hemisphere.
That is the usual method of diverting attention
from the main issue before the Council . . . Mr.
Lodge remarked that he would prefer that the
Security Council should refrain from considering
aggression when it occurred in the Western Hemisphere, that is, that he wanted the United
States to be left alone with all the backward
countries in Latin America . . ."

d. Vote: a general resolution against continuation of any
action likely to cause bloodshed, or assistance thereto,
was passed unanimously, following the Soviet veto of
a Brazilian-Colombian resolution to refer the matter
to the Organization of American States.

3. The Guatemalan government that had lodged the com-
plaints collapsed before the OAS could act, and the case
became moot at both the UN and the OAS.

4. Repercussions.

C. Cuba, 1960-October ?, 1962: The Problem of Proof.

1. The Seventh Meeting of Consultation, San Jose, August
16-28, 1960: resulted in a Declaration condemning extra-
continental intervention and the Sino-Soviet efforts to
exploit political, economic, and social situations in any
American state but without direct censure of Cuba or any
arrangement for collective measures.

2. Punta del Este. 1962: an appraisal of the "juridical"
versus the plenary-power concepts of the competence of
the Organ of Consultation. Notes on the Resolutions and
the voting record.

3. The Washington Conversations, October 2-3, 1962.

IV. The Law and the Cuban Crisis After October 22, 1962.

A. The situation as of October 28, 1962: The Steps That Were
Taken.

64

B. Measures not involved in legal controversy or uncertainty.

1. Severance of diplomatic relations.

2. Cutting off advantages and trade.

3. Closing United States ports to ships and shipping lines engaged in carriage of supplies to Cuba.

4. Exclusion of the present government of Cuba from participation in the inter-American system: no longer controversial even though voted 14-1 (Cuba) with 6 abstentions at Punta del Este.

5. Cooperative intelligence and related security measures against subversive activities in the Americas.

6. Others?

C. The legality of the quarantine voted by the OAS.

1. Under the customary law of visitation and search and of port blockade.

2. Deployment and possible use of seapower: a collective measure of self-defense under the Rio Pact and the OAS Charter? Under the UN Charter? The problem of anticipatory self-defense versus unauthorized use of force.

D. The powers of the United Nations to take provisional measures with regard to missile capabilities in Cuba.

1. The United States proposal.

2. Powers of the Security Council.

3. Powers of the General Assembly: is a favorable recommendation effective as a legal authorization for U.S.-OAS use of force to dismantle or interdict the missile bases?

4. OAS-or U.S. action: legal authority of the UN to control or restrain?

E. The problem not yet touched in the actions to date: use of force in Cuba and elsewhere with regard to the threats to peace created by Soviet political and military presence in Cuba and by the hostile orientation and attitude of the Castro regime.

1. Status after the events of October 22-26 of the earlier reservation of the United States' position as to unilateral action under the "fight if we must" resolution of Congress and Presidential declarations.

2. UN powers: see A-3, above.

3. US-OAS powers without UN authorization.

    a. Self-defense?

    b. Consistent with Articles 2-4 of the UN Charter?

    c. Extent of the OAS commitment to collective measures.

4. Some possible conditioning factors:

    a. What authority is in control of the bomber-aircraft in Cuba?

    b. The possibility that the build-up was for enticement of invasion (USSR versus Cuba?).

    c. Possible drives for reciprocal concessions:

        (i)   As to dismantling of certain installations.

        (ii) As to effective withdrawal of presences from "sections of predominant interest."

    d. Estimates of responses to use of force in Cuba.

F. The Hope of October 28, 1962: Escalation for Peace and Security.

Appendix B

ORGANIZATION OF AMERICAN STATES

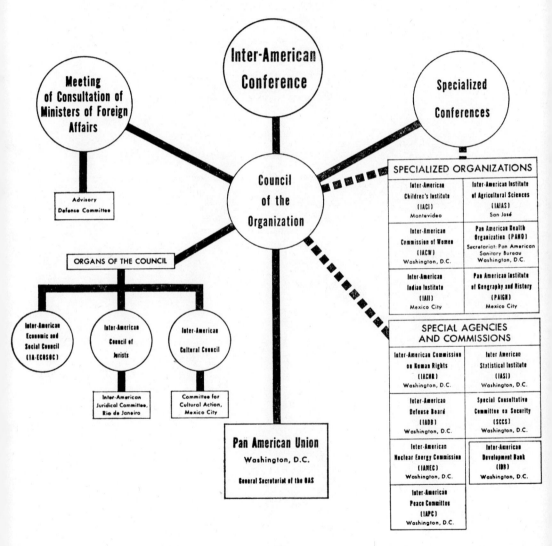

Inter-American Conference

Meeting of Consultation of Ministers of Foreign Affairs

Specialized Conferences

Council of the Organization

Advisory Defense Committee

ORGANS OF THE COUNCIL

Inter-American Economic and Social Council (IA-ECOSOC)

Inter-American Council of Jurists

Inter-American Cultural Council

Inter-American Juridical Committee, Rio de Janeiro

Committee for Cultural Action, Mexico City

Pan American Union
Washington, D.C.
General Secretariat of the OAS

SPECIALIZED ORGANIZATIONS

Inter-American Children's Institute (IACI) Montevideo	Inter-American Institute of Agricultural Sciences (IAIAS) San José
Inter-American Commission of Women (IACW) Washington, D.C.	Pan American Health Organization (PAHO) Secretariat: Pan American Sanitary Bureau Washington, D.C.
Inter-American Indian Institute (IAII) Mexico City	Pan American Institute of Geography and History (PAIGH) Mexico City

SPECIAL AGENCIES AND COMMISSIONS

Inter-American Commission on Human Rights (IACHR) Washington, D.C.	Inter American Statistical Institute (IASI) Washington, D.C.
Inter-American Defense Board (IADB) Washington, D.C.	Special Consultative Committee on Security (SCCS) Washington, D.C.
Inter-American Nuclear Energy Commission (IANEC) Washington, D.C.	Inter-American Development Bank (IDB) Washington, D.C.
Inter-American Peace Committee (IAPC) Washington, D.C.	

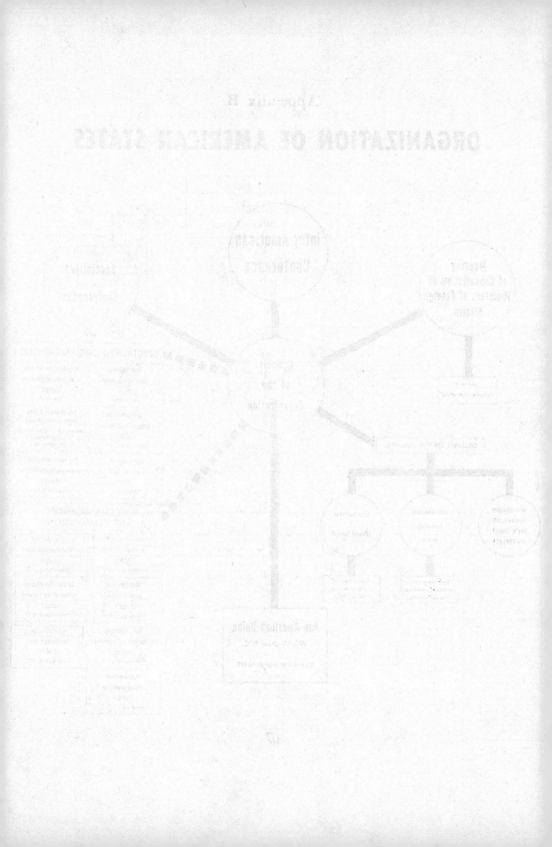

Appendix C

PAN AMERICAN UNION

Permanent and Central Organ and General Secretariat
of the Organization of American States

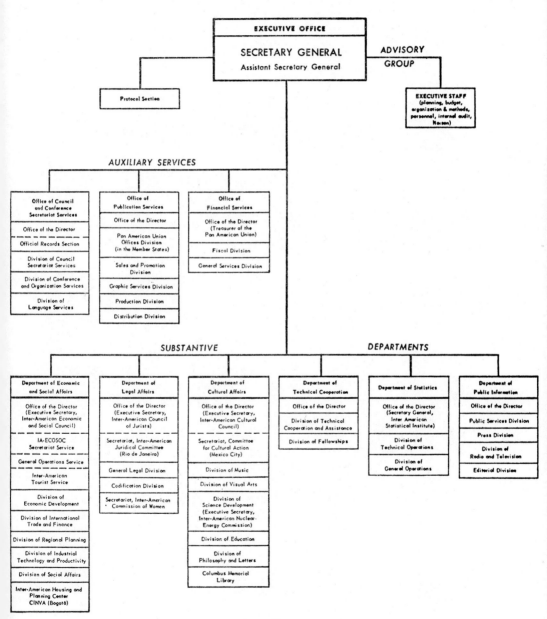

BIBLIOGRAPHY

SELECTED BIBLIOGRAPHY
ON THE CUBAN CRISIS*

DOCUMENTARY SOURCES

American foreign ministers condemn Sino-Soviet intervention in American states: three statements made by Secretary Herter at the seventh meeting of consultation of the American foreign ministers at San José, Costa Rica; together with the text of a declaration adopted by the ministers on Aug. 28, 1960 . . . Sept. 12, 1960. 43 Dep't State Bull. 395-409.

Charter of Punta del Este (in U.S. Administrative law. Legislation on foreign relations with explanatory notes. Washington, 1962, pp. 543-55).

Communications de l'organisation des états américains et de Cuba; requête de Cuba contre les Etats-Unis. 1961. 10 (1) Rev. des Nations Unies 5-14.

Cuba (in summary of the general debate). Nov. 1960. 7 U.N. Rev. 46-8.

Cuba charges U.S. with imminent military aggression. 1961. 8 (2) U.N. Rev. 26-31.

Cuba. Dep't of Public Relations. In defense of national sovereignty. Havana. 1959. 23p.

Cuba. Ministry of Foreign Relations. Reply to U.S.A.: Cuba is a sovereign nation by its own right not by any grant. Osvaldo Dorticos Tarrado. Havana. 1960. 10p. (Radio and television address, Jan. 27, 1960).

Cuba, Ministerio de Relaciones Exteriores. Dep. de Relaciones Públicas. Una nueva diplomacia. Habana. 1959. 35p.

Cuba. Secretaría de Estado. Cuba replies to the U.S.A. note: in defense of national sovereignty. Habana, 1959. 23p.

Cuba's reply to the note of the United States of America. Cuba, Univ. de Oriente, Departamento de extensión y relaciones culturales. No. 55. 1960. 25p.

Inter-American conference for the maintenance of continental peace and security. Rio de Janeiro, Aug. 15-Sept. 2, 1947. Washington. 1960. 7p. (English, OEA/Ser./A/1).

Inter-American Conference, 11th, Quito, 1961. General Secretariat. Latinoamérica y el derecho internacional americano. 1959. 150p.

---

* Prepared by the Library of The Association of the Bar of the City of New York under the direction of Joseph L. Andrews, Reference Librarian.

73

Inter-American Council of Jurists. Inter-American Juridical Committee.

Instrument relating to violations of the principles of non-intervention. Draft and report prepared in accordance with res. VII, fifth meeting of consultation . . . Washington, Pan American Union. 1959. 29p.

Opinion on the legal aspects of the draft declaration on nonintervention presented by the Mexican delegation. Prepared in accordance with res. V, fifth meeting of consultation . . . Washington, Pan American Union. 1961. 29p.

Opinion on the scope of the powers of the Council of the organization of American states. Prepared in accordance with resolution of April 21, 1949 . . . and with res. III, 1st meeting of consultation . . . Washington, Pan American Union, 1961. 21p.

Study . . . of the proposal of Ecuador concerning the Inter-American peace committee (Chap. 1, topic 4c of the agenda). Washington, Pan American Union. 1960.

Study of the proposal of Ecuador concerning the Inter-American peace committee. Prepared in accordance with res. VI, fifth meeting . . . of consultation . . . Washington, Pan American Union. 1960. 11p.

Inter-American Peace Committee. Report to the eighth meeting of consultation of ministers of foreign affairs. Washington, Pan American Union. 1962. v.p. (OEA/Ser.L/III/CIP/1/62 (English)).

Kennedy, John F. The lesson of Cuba. May 8, 1961. 44 Dep't State Bull. 659-61.

Manning, William Ray. Diplomatic correspondence of the United States concerning the independence of the Latin American nations; selected and arranged . . . New York, Oxford Univ. Press. 1925. 3v.

Meeting of Consultation of Ministers of Foreign Affairs of American States, Sixth, San José, Costa Rica, 1960.

Cuba en la OEA; VI y VII reuniones de consulta de ministros de relaciones exteriores . . . 16 al 29 de agosto de 1960. Habana, Impr. Nacional de Cuba. 1960. 164p.

Doc. 1-82 (English). San José. 1960. (OEA/ser.F./#7).

Final act. Washington, Pan American Union. 1960. 9p.

Final act. Washington, Pan American Union. 1960. 36p. (OEA/Ser.C./II. 7 (English)).

No action on Cuba's complaint against the United States. March 1962. 9 U.N. Rev. 13-15.

Organization of American States. Council.

Regulations of the meeting of consultation of ministers of foreign affairs. Approved by the council . . . March 1, 1951. The temporary provisions applicable to the seventh meeting . . . were approved . . . Aug. 8, 1960. Washington, Pan American Union. 1960. 6p. (OEA/Ser.F./I.1 (English)) JX1980.35.A231. 1951.

Regulations of the meeting of consultation of ministers of foreign affairs, to serve as organ of consultation in application of the inter-American treaty of reciprocal assistance. Washington, Pan American Union. 1960. 10p. (OEA/Ser.F./I.2 (English)) JX 1980.356.A231.

Organization of American States.
Fifth meeting of consultation of ministers of foreign affairs, Santiago, Chile, Aug. 12-18, 1959: final act. Washington, Pan American Union. 1960. (OEA/Ser.C./II.5).
Eighth meeting of consultation of ministers of foreign affairs, Punta del Este, Uruguay, Jan. 22-31, 1962: final act. 1962. 20p. (OEA/Ser.C/II.8).

Pan American Union.
Documentos oficiales de la organización de los Estados americanos: índice y lista general. Vol. I—. 1960—. Washington. 1961—.
Dep't of International Law. Manual of inter-American relations; a systematic classification of the treaties, conventions, resolutions adopted at Inter-American conference, 1956. Conf. Ser. 42. 344p.
Dep't of Legal Affairs. The organization of American states and the United Nations. Manuel Canyes. 1960. 63p.
General Legal Division. Application of the inter-American treaty of reciprocal assistance, 1948-56; with a discussion of the inter-American system of peace and security and its operation within the world system. Washington. 1957. 247p.
Inter-American Juridical Comm. Contribution of the American continent to the principles of international law that govern the responsibility of the state. 1962.
Legal Division. Inter-American treaties and conventions, signatures, ratifications and deposits with explanatory notes. Rev. ed. Washington. 1961. (Treaty Ser. no. 9).

Reply to U.S. state department white paper on Cuba. Defensa Institucional Cubana. 1961. 15p.

Responsibility of Cuban government for increased international tensions in the hemisphere. Aug. 29, 1960. 43 Dep't State Bull. 318-46.

Rusk, Dean. Report to the nation on the Punta del Este conference. 1962. 46 Dep't State Bull. 267-9.

Security council considers Cuban complaint: text of statements made by U.S. Rep. Henry Cabot Lodge and a resolution adopted on July 19, 1960. Aug. 8, 1960. 43 Dep't State Bull. 199-205.

Stevenson, Adlai E. U.N. security council rejects Cuban call for opinion of world court on OAS action. 1962. 46 Dep't State Bull. 684-94.

Stevenson, Adlai E. and Plimpton, Francis T. P. U.N. general assembly rejects Cuban charges against United States. 1962. 46 Dep't State Bull. 553-61.

Text of the communique issued by foreign ministers of 20 countries in western hemisphere at close of two day conference on Cuba and the threat of communism. New York Times, Oct. 4, 1962, p. 10.

Text of Kennedy's address on moves to meet the Soviet buildup in Cuba. New York Times, Oct. 23, 1962, p. 18.

United Nations. General Assembly. Complaint by the revolutionary government of Cuba regarding the various plans of aggression and acts of intervention being executed by the government of the United States of America against the government of Cuba, constituting a manifest violation of its territorial integrity, sovereignty and independence, and a clear threat to international peace and security; letter dated March 17, 1961 from the chairman of the delegation of Guatemala to the president of the general assembly. New York. 1960. 7p. (1961. A/4710).

United Nations. Security Council.
Letter dated 15 July 1960 from the permanent representative of the United States of America addressed to the president of the security council; transmitting a memorandum, June 27, 1960 . . . entitled *Provocative actions of the government of Cuba against the United States which have served to increase tensions in the Caribbean area.* New York. 1960. 12p. (1960.S/4388).

Security council debate ends with no resolution adopted—Cuba charges U.S. with imminent military aggression—U.S. rejects complaint: calls it fraudulent. Feb. 1961. 8 U.N. Rev. 26-31.

Security council rejects Cuba's request. April 1962. 9 U.N. Rev. 14-17.

United States and Soviet Union exchange messages in regard to events in Cuba. May 8, 1961. 44 Dep't State Bull. 661-7.

U.S. Congress. House. Comm. on Foreign Affairs.
Expressing the sense of the Congress relative to the reevaluation of the role of the government of Cuba in inter-American affairs. Report. Washington. 1961. 2p.
(87.2) Regional and other documents concerning United States relations with Latin America. Washington. 1962. 204p.

U.S. Congress. Senate. Comm. on Foreign Relations.
(81.1) A decade of American foreign policy; basic documents 1941-49 . . . Washington. 1950. (Sen. doc. 123) Part V, The inter-American system, pp. 411-53.
(86.1) United States-Latin American relations: the Organization of American states. 1959. 87p. (Prep. by Northwestern univ.)

United States Delegation to the General Assembly. Statement by Francis T. P. Plimpton; statement by Adlai E. Stevenson. Press release, 3925, 3927, 3928, 3929.

U.S. Department of State. Bur. of Pub. Affairs. Off. of Pub. Serv. Cuba. Washington. 1961. 36p. (Dep't of state pub. 7171; inter-American series 66)

Wadsworth, James J. and Barco, J.W. United Nations security council fears Cuban complaint against United States, adjourns without a vote. 1961. 44 Dep't State Bull. 104-14.

BOOKS AND PAMPHLETS

General

Acuna, Juan Antonio. Cuba: revolución traicionada; Fidel hoy entregado al comunismo que fué aliado de Batista ayer; documentos irrefutables de la alianza del comunismo con el tirano Batista y de la traición de Fidel Castro. Montevideo, Edit. "Goes". 1962. 168p.

Alexander, Robert J. Prophets of the revolution. New York, Macmillan. 1962. 322p.

American Assembly. The United States and Latin America; background papers and the final report of the sixteenth assembly, Arden House, Harriman, N.Y., Oct. 15-18, 1959. Final ed. New York. 1959. 221p.

Benitez, Jaime. The U.S., Cuba and Latin America; an occasional paper on the free society. Santa Barbara, Calif., Center for the Study of Democratic Institutions. 1961. 10p.

Berle, Adolf A. Jr. Latin America; diplomacy and reality. New York, Harper & Row (for Council on Foreign Relations). 1962.

Caicedo Castilla, José Joaquín. El panamericanismo. Buenos Aires, R. Depalma. 1961. 484p.

Castro, Fidel. 4 horas anti-imperialistas en la ONU. Lima, Edit. Libertad. 1961. 127p.

History will absolve me: tr. from the Spanish of a defense plea by Fidel Castro. New York, Lyle Stuart Pub. 1961. 79p.

The only lawful guarantee of our power. 1962. 8 Int'l Aff. (Moscow) 63-71.

Casuso, Teresa. Cuba and Castro; tr. from the Spanish by Elmer Grossberg. New York, Random House. 1961. 249p.

Cuba, its people, its society, its culture. Wyatt MacGaffey and Clifford R. Barnett. Prep. under the auspices of the American University. New Haven, HRAF Press. 1962.

Cuba-United States relations (chronologies). New York, International Review Service. 1962.

De Madariaga, Salvador. Latin America between the eagle and the bear. New York, Praeger, 1962. 192p.

Dozer, Donald Marquand. Are we good neighbors? Three decades of inter-American relations 1930-1960. Gainesville, Univ. of Florida Press. 1959.

Draper, T. Castro's revolution. New York, Praeger, 1962. 218p.

Foner, P. S. A history of Cuba and its relations with the United States. Vol. 1, International Pub. 1962.

Frank, W. D. Cuba, prophetic island. New York, Marzani & Munsell. 1962. 191p.

Graber, Doris Appel. Crisis diplomacy; a history of U.S. intervention policies and practices. Washington, Public Affairs Press. 1959. 402p.

James, Daniel. Cuba, el primer satélite soviético en América . . . Mexico, Libreros Mexicanos Unidos. 1962. 391p.

Julien, Claude. La revolución cubana. Montevideo, Ediciones Marcha. 1961. 259p.

Kirk, Grayson L. The Monroe doctrine today. New York, Toronto, Farrar & Rhinehart. 1941. 32p.

Lieuwen, E. Arms and politics in Latin America. Rev. ed. New York, Praeger (for the Council of Foreign Relations). 1961. 335p.

Manger, William. Pan America in crisis; the future of the OAS. With an introd. by Alberto Lleras Camargo and foreword by Hector David Castro. Washington, Public Affairs Press. 1961. 104p.

Matthew, Herbert L. The Cuban story. New York, Braziller. 1961. 318p.

Meyer, K. E. and Szulc, Tad. The Cuban invasion. New York, Praeger, 1962.

Mezerik, Avrahm G. Cuba and the United States: record of revolution, USSR-China, U.N. and OAS action. New York, 1960. 49p.

Miller, Warren. 90 miles from home; the face of Cuba today. Boston, Little, Brown. 1961. 279p.

Mills, C. Wright. Listen, Yankee; the revolution in Cuba. New York, McGraw-Hill. 1960. 192p.

Ortiz de Zevallos, Javier. América frente a la intervención colectiva auspicida. Lima. 1947. 91p.

Palmer, Thomas Waverly. Search for a Latin American policy. Gainesville, Univ. of Florida Press. 1957. 217p.

Perkins, Dexter. The United States and Latin America. Baton Rouge, Louisiana State Univ. Press. 1961. 124p.

Porter, Charles O. The struggle for democracy in Latin America. New York, Macmillan. 1961. 215p.

Prada, Jaime Luz Marina. Paralelo entre la ONU y OEA; solución pacífica de las controversias. Bogotá. 1960. 93p.

Rivero, Nicolas. Castro's Cuba. Washington, Robert B. Luce. 1962. 239p.

Smith, R. F. The United States and Cuba: business and diplomacy 1917-60. New York, Bookman Associates. 1961. 256p.

Szulc, Tad. The winds of revolution. Latin America today and tomorrow. New York, Praeger. 1962. 300p.

Tannenbaum, Frank.
    The American tradition in foreign policy. Norman, Univ. of Oklahoma Press. 1955. 178p.
    Peace by revolution; an interpretation of Mexico. New York, Columbia Univ. Press. 1933. 316p.
    Ten keys to Latin America. New York, Knopf. 1962. 237p.

Vann, Carl R., ed. American policy and the Cuban revolution. Syracuse, Syracuse Univ., Maxwell Grad. School of Citizenship & Public Affairs. 1961. 95p.

Weyl, Nathaniel.
    Red star over Cuba. New York, Devin-Adair. 1960. 222p.

La estrella roja sobre Cuba; el asalto soviético al hemisferio occidental. Buenos Aires, Edit. Freeland. 1961. 221p.

Whitaker, Arthur P.
Las Américas y un mundo en crisis. Traducción de Ernesto Montenegro. Lancaster, Pa., Lancaster Press. 1946. 366p.
Development of American regionalism; the Organization of American states. March 1951. 469 Int'l Conciliation 121-64.
The western hemisphere idea: its rise and decline. Ithaca, Cornell Univ. Press. 1954. 194p.

Zanotti, Isidoro. Organizacao des estados americanos. Rio de Janeiro. 1948. 104p.

Legal

Alvarado Garaicoa, Teodoro. Los principios internacionales de no intervención y autodeterminación. La Haya, Dijkman. 1962. 78p.

Alvarado, Rafael, ed. Los principales instrumentos; síntesis de derecho internacional americano. Compilación y notas. Quito, Casa de la Cultura Ecuatoriana. 1960. 172p.

Alvarez, Alejandro. The Monroe doctrine in the international life of the states of the new world. New York, Oxford Univ. Press. 1924. 573p.

Bishop, William W., Jr. International law, cases and materials. Boston, Little, Brown. 1962. pp. 744-83.

Blackman, Henry M. United States policy and the inter-American peace system, 1889-1952. Paris. 1952. 221p.

Bradley, Phillips. A bibliography of the Monroe doctrine 1919-1929. Letchworth, Printed by the Garden City Press Ltd.; London, Pub. by the London School of Economics. 1929. 39p.

Buuren, H. van. The Monroe doctrine and manifest destiny (in Symbolae Verzijl, La Haye, 1958, pp. 101-17).

Canyes Santacana, Manuel. The Organization of American states and the United Nations. 5th ed. Washington, Pan American Union. 1960. 63p.

Dreier, John C. The organization of American states and the hemisphere crisis. New York, Harper & Row (for the Council on Foreign Relations). 1962.

Fabela, Isidro.
Las doctrinas Monroe y Drago. Mexico, Univ. Nacional Autónoma de México, Escuela Nacional de Ciencias Políticas y Sociales. 1957. 266p.
Intervención. México, Escuela Nacional de Ciencias Políticas y Sociales. 1959. 376p.

Fernández-Shaw, Félix G. La organización de los estados americanos. Madrid, Ediciones Cultura Hispánica. 1959. 770p.

Freeman, Alwyn V. The political powers of the OAS council (in Lipsky, George A., ed., Law and politics in the world community. Berkeley, Univ. of California Press. 1953. pp. 252-78).

Godoy, Gastón. El caso cubano y la organización de estados americanos. Madrid, O.E.A. 1961. 110p.

Gomez Valle, Sara. La no intervención en los estados americanos. México. 1949. 70p.

Guillén Atienza, Luis. El principio de no intervención y las doctrinas americanas. Santiago de Chile. 1949. 223p. (Colección de estudios de derecho internacional. V.7).

Hackworth, Green Haywood. Digest of international law . . . Washington, Gov't Print. Off. 1943. Vol. V, pp. 435-70.

Hoyo Algara, Francisco del. Estudio de la organización de los estados americanos. Mexico. 1952. 108p.

Hughes, Charles Evans. Pan American peace plans. New Haven, Yale Univ. Press, 1929. 68p.

Hyde, Charles Cheney. International law, chiefly as interpreted and applied by the United States . . . 2d rev. ed. Boston, Little, Brown, 1945. (Intervention, vol. 1, pp. 245-81; Monroe doctrine, vol. 1, pp. 281-318; blockade, Vol. 3, pp. 2177-2223).

López-Jiménez, Ramón. El principio de no intervención en América y la nota uruguaya. Buenos Aires, Depalma. 1947.

Maúrtua, Víctor Manuel. Intervención-conciliación-arbitraje en las conferencias de la Habana, 1928 y Washington, 1929. Habana, Impr. Molina y Cía. 1929. 196p.

Mecham, John Lloyd. The United States and inter-American security, 1889-1960. Austin, Univ. of Texas Press. 1961. 514p.

Monroy, G. Oscar. El estado de paz en el derecho internacional. Mexico. 1952. 134p.

Munguia Araújo, Carlos N. Intervención. León, Nicaragua. 1945. 56p.

Nawaz, M. K. Intervention by invitation and the U.N. charter. New Delhi. 1959. 7p.

Oppenheim, L. F. L.
International law: a treatise. 8th ed. ed. by H. Lauterpacht. London, Longmans, Green. 1955. (Vol. 1, Intervention, pp. 304-20). 7th ed. 1952. (Vol 2, Blockade, pp. 767-97).

Perkins, Dexter. A history of the Monroe doctrine. Rev. ed. Boston, Little, Brown. 1955. 462p.

Planas-Suárez, Simón. Les principes américains de politique internationale et la doctrine de Monroe. Bâle, Berlag fur Recht und Gesellschaft. 1960. 244p.

Rojas, Galdames René. Organización de los estados americanos. Santiago, Editorial Jurídica de Chile. 1951. pp. 396-436.

Rousseau, Charles E. Relations internationales. Paris, Cours de Droit. 1950. 2v.

Ruiz Ruiz, Ramón. Doctrina de Monroe. León, Nicaragua. 1949. 56p. (Tesis, Univ. de Nicaragua).

Sepúlveda César. La Teoría y la Práctica del Reconocimiento de Gobiernos (1954).

Smyrdadis, Bion. La intervención ante la corte internacional de justicia. Buenos Aires, 1954. 6p.

Stone, Julius. Aggression and World Order; a critique of United Nations Theories of Aggression. Berkeley, University of California Press, 1958. 226p.

Stone, Julius. Legal controls of international conflict. 2d impression, rev. with supplement 1953-58. New York, Rinehart. 1959. 903p.

Stowell, Ellery Cory. Intervention in international law. Washington. J. Byrne & Co. 1921. 558p.

Teslanko, Nicolas. Le domaine réservé et le conseil de sécurité. Paris, Univ. de Paris. 1950. 253p.

Thomas, Ann van Wynen and Thomas, A. J., Jr.
Non-intervention; the law and its import in the America. Dallas, Southern Methodist Univ. Press. 1956. 476p.
The Organization of American states. Dallas, Southern Methodist Univ. Press. 1962.

Trelles y Govin, Carlos Manuel. Estudio de la bibliografía cubana sobre la doctrina de Monroe . . . Habana, "El Siglo XX". 1922. 234p.

U.S. Library of Congress. Div. of Bibliography. List of references on the Monroe doctrine. Compiled under the direction of Herman H. B. Meyer. Washington, Gov't Print. Off. 1919. 122p.

Wilson, Larman C. The principle of non-intervention in inter-American relations. Doctoral dissertation in preparation, Univ. of Maryland.

PERIODICAL REFERENCES

General

After four years of Castro—Cuba today. Oct. 22, 1962. 60 Newsweek 35, 38.

Berle, Adolf A., Jr. The Cuban crisis: failure of American foreign policy. 1960. 39 For. Aff. 40-55.

Bernucci, G. L. A Punta del Este né vinti; né vincitori. Feb. 1962. 13 Esteri 9-10, 15-28.

La conférence de Punta del Este, 22-31 janvier 1962. Feb. 1962. 18 Perspectives VIII/1-5, 17.

Connell-Smith, G. The future of the Organization of American states—significance of the Punta del Este conference. March 1962. 18 World Today 112-20.

Durable doctrine. Sept. 21, 1962. 80 Time 17-21.

Facio Gonzalo, J. O desarmamento como fator de desenvolvimento económico na america latina. Junho 1958. 1 (2) Rev. Brasileira de Política Internacional 29-44.

Ferguson, J. Halcro. The Cuban revolution and Latin America. July 1961. 37 Int'l Aff. 285-92.

Fitzgibbon, Russell H. The revolution next door: Cuba, 1961. 334 Annals 113-22.

Fitzgibbon, Russell H. and Johnson, K. F. Measurement of Latin

American political change. Sept. 1961. 55 Am. Pol. Sci. Rev. 515-26.

Goldenberg, B. South of Cuba—Latin America in the Soviet mirror. July/Sept. 1961. Survey, a journal of Soviet & E. European Studies 12-17.

Graber, Doris Appel. United States intervention in Latin America. 1962. 16 Yb. World Aff. 23-50.

Hulsey, R. H. Cuban revolution: its impact on American foreign policy. 1960. 14 J. Int'l Aff. 158-74.

Johnson, P. Caribbean Suez? July 9, 1960. 60 New Statesman 43-44.

Martillo, T. The Bankruptcy of Washington's Latin American policy. June 1961. 7 Int'l Aff. (Moscow) 15-20.

Moley, Raymond. Monroe doctrine today. Newsweek, Sept. 24, and Oct. 1, 1962.

Monroe doctrine; past and present. Sept. 10, 1962. 53 U.S. News 44.

Monroe to Kennedy: death of a doctrine? Sept. 24, 1962. 53 U.S. News 44.

Peralta-Peralta, J. Aportes para una revisión del concepto del mundo hispánico. Enero-febrero 1961. Rev. de Estudios Políticos 103-37.

Quarantine for Cuba. Oct. 22, 1960. 197 Economist 350.

Szulc, Tad.
    OAS opens talk about Cuba today. Foreign ministers to begin two day Washington parley. New York Times, Oct. 2, 1962, p. 15.
    U.S. ports to bar ships that carry arms aid to Cuba. New York Times, Oct. 4, 1962, pp. 1, 11.
    U.S. tells Latins it will take lead to counter reds—Rusk, at talk on Cuba issue, stresses political efforts—meeting ends today. New York Times, Oct. 3, 1962, pp. 1, 3.

Tannenbaum, Frank.
    Castro and social change. 1962. 77 Pol. Sci. Q. 178-204.
    The United States and Latin America. June 1961. 76 Pol. Sci. Q. 161-80.

U.S. Department of State. Bureau of Public Affairs. Cuban responsibility in increased tensions in the hemisphere. 1960. 43 Dep't State Bull. 317-49.

Veilly, M. Cuba et les Amériques. 1961. 17 Rev. de Défense Nationale 808-18.

Vernant, J. A Punta del Este—les états-unis et l'Amérique latine. March 1962. 18 Rev. de Défense Nationale 527-34.

Washington denuncia il regime di Castro. 1961. 25 Relaziono Internaz. 453-7.

What should Monroe doctrine mean? Blockade. Sept. 21, 1962. 53 Life 4.

Legal

Accioly, Hildebrando. O princípio de naointervencao e a convencao de Havana sobre lutas civis. 1949. Inter-Am. Jurid. Yb. 3-8.

Ball, M. M. Issue for the Americas: non-intervention v. human rights and the preservation of democratic institutions. 1961. 15 Int'l Org. 21-37.

Barratt, J. Arthur. The real Monroe doctrine. 1929. 14 Grotius Soc'y 1-27.

Bayona Ortiz, Antonio. Aspectos político-jurídicos de la organización internacional americana. Bogotá, Impr. del Departamento. 1953. 131p.

Díaz Doin, G. La organización de estados americanos y la no intervención. May/June 1960. 19 (3) Cuadernos Americanos 73-88.

Dreier, John C. The OAS and the Cuban crisis. Winter 1961. 5 SAIS Rev. 3-8.

Dupuy, R. J. Organisation internationale et unité politique—la crise de l'organisation des états américains. 1960. 6 Ann. Francais de Droit Internationale 185-224.

Facio, Gonzalo J. El reconocimiento como institución jurídica americana al servicio de la democracia. San José, Impr. Falco. 1952-24p.

Falk, Richard A.
American intervention in Cuba and the rule of law. 1961. 22 Ohio St. L. J. 546-85.
The United States and the doctrine of nonintervention in the internal affairs of independent states. 1959. 5 How. L. J. 163-89.

Fawcett, J. E. S. Intervention in international law; a study of some recent cases. 1961. 103 Recueil des Cours, v. 2, 347-421.

Fenwick, Charles G.
The competence of the council of the organization of American states. 1949. Inter-Am. Jurid. Yb. 21-39.
Inter-American regional procedures for the settlement of disputes. 1956. 10 Int'l Org. 12-21.
The inter-American system of collective security. 1960. 8 Acad. Inter-americana de Derecho Comparado e Internacional, Cursos monográficos. 57-100.
Intervention and the inter-American rule of law. 1959. 53 Am. J. Int'l L. 873-6.
Intervention: individual and collective, 1945. 39 Am. J. Int'l L. 645-63.
The issues at Punta del Este: non-intervention v. collective security. 1962. 56 Am. J. Int'l L. 469-74.

Friedmann, W. For restraint toward Cuba. Letter to the New York Times dated Oct. 12, 1962. New York Times, Oct. 16, 1962, p. 38.

Fuchs, Gilles. La commission interaméricaine de la paix. 1957. 3 Ann. Francais de Droit International 142-9.

García-Mora, Manuel R. International law and the law of hostile military expeditions. 1958. 27 Fordham L. Rev. 309-31.

Godoy, Horacio H.
International law and the new movement in Latin America. 1960. 54 Am. Soc'y Int'l L. Proc. 96-101.

Remarks on "intervention" and the Cuban case. 1961. 55 Am. Soc'y Int'l L. Proc. 24-7.

Lacarte, Julio A. The Latin American system. 1959. 53 Am. Soc'y Int'l L. Proc. 62-8.

Lador-Lederer, J. J.
Intervention—a historical stocktaking. 1959. 29 Nordisk Tidsshrift für Int'l Recht 127.
Zenith and decay of the doctrine of non-intervention of states in the internal affairs of other states. Aug. 1958. 5 (11) Congrès Int'l de Droit Comparé, Rapports Généraux 921.

Larson, A. The Cuban incident and the rule of law. May 13, 1961. 44 Saturday Review 28, 53.

Mora, José A. The organization of American states. Autumn 1960. 14 Int'l Org. 514-23.

Murdock, James Oliver and Gobbi, Hugo J. The inter-American juridical committee. 1960. 9 Am. J. Comp. L. 596-605.

Nizard, Lucien. La question Cubaine devant le Conseil de Sécurité. 1962. 66 Revue Générale de Droit International Public 486-545.

Reeves, W. H. The Cuban situation (in New York state bar ass'n. comm. on int'l law. Report. 1961, pp. 1-8).

Rendón, G. García. L'Organisation des republiques américaines et le maintien de la paix. Bruxelles, Le Droit au Service de la Paix, Déc. 1957, no. 2.

Ronning, C. Neale. Intervention, international law, and the inter-American system. 1961. 3 J. Inter-Am. Studies 249-71.

Thomas, A. J., Jr.
Non-intervention and public order in the Americas. 1959. 53 Am. Soc'y Int'l L. Proc. 72-80.
The Organization of American states and subversive intervention. 1961. 55 Am. Soc'y Int'l L. Proc. 19-24.

Thomas, A. J., Jr. and Thomas, A. V. W. Democracy and the organization of American states. 1961. 46 Minn. L. Rev. 337.

Travis, Martin B., Jr. The political and social bases for the Latin American doctrine of non-intervention. 1959. 53 Am. Soc'y Int'l L. Proc. 68-72.

Waldock, C. H. M. The regulation of the use of force by individual states in international law. 81 Recueil des Cours 455-514.

Wright, Quincy.
Intervention and Cuba in 1961. 1961. 55 Am. Soc'y Int'l L. Proc. 2-19.
Subversive intervention. 1960. 54 Am. J. Int'l L. 521-35.

SUPPLEMENT TO THE BIBLIOGRAPHY

(June 1, 1963)

Arnault, Jacques. Cuba et le marxisme. Paris. 1963. 206p.

Aron, R. International law: reality and fiction. Dec. 1, 1962. 147 New Republic (Washington) 13-14.

Baciu, Stefan. Cortina de hierro sobre Cuba. Prefacio de Salvador de Madariaga. Buenos Aires, Edit. San Isidro. 1961. 210p.

Bartossová, M. The United States aggression against Cuba from the view-point of international law (in Czech). 1963. 102 Právník, 24-37.

Berle, Adolf A., Jr. The Cuban crisis (in Gyorgy, A. and Gibbs, H. S. Problems in international relations. 2d. ed. Englewood Cliffs, N. J. 1962. pp. 140-55).

Bernhard Indarte, Guillermo y Etchepare, A. Reportaje a Cuba. Montevideo, Ediciones América Nueva. 1961. 190p.

Blanco, Enrique José. De playa Girón a Punta del Este. Buenos Aires. 1962. 94p.

Carranza, A. Romero. Excepciones legítimas y legales al principio de no intervención. Sept. 28, 1961. 23 Jurisprudencia Argentina 1.

Castro, Fidel. La revolución cubana. Buenos Aires, Editorial Palestra. 1960. 476p. (Colección Vertientes de la libertad).

Chayes, Abram. The legal case for U.S. action on Cuba. 1962. 47 Dep't State Bull. 763-5.

Critical situation in Caribbean urgently considered by security council. 1962. 9 (11) U.N. Rev. 6-17.

Cuba: from protests to removal of Soviet missiles. 1962. 14 (43) Current Digest of the Soviet Press 3-15.

The Cuban crisis in perspective. Dec. 1962. 14 Monthly Rev. 401-13.

Daniel, James and Hubbell, John G. Strike in the west, the complete story of the Cuban crisis. New York, Holt, Rinehart and Winston. 1963. 180p.

Eisenhower, Milton S. The wine is bitter: the United States and Latin America. Garden City, N. Y., Doubleday. 1963.

Elizalde, Leopoldo Pío, ed. Tres años; introducción, notas y epílogo de Leopoldo Pío Elizalde. México, Ed. Botas. 1962. 687p.

Fabela, Isidro. El caso de Cuba. México, Ed. Cuadernos Americanos. 1960. 87p.

Fagen, R. R. Calculation and emotion in foreign policy—the Cuban case. 1962. 6 J. Conflict Resolution 214-21.

Foreign Policy Association. The Cuban crisis: a documentary record. New York. 1963. 84p.

Freeman, Thomas, pseud. The crisis in Cuba. Derby, Conn., Monarch. 1963. 159p.

Gardner, Richard N. The United Nations in crisis: Cuba and the Congo. 1963. 48 Dep't State Bull. 477-81.

Guilbert, Yves. El "infidel" Castro; el polvorín cubano. México, Plaza & Janés y Edit. Herrero. 1961. 220p.

Haerdter, R. Monroe-Doktrin und Kuba-krise. Nov. 1962. 13 Aussenpolitik 735-41.

Halpern, Manfred. The morality and politics of intervention. New York, Council on Religion and International Affairs. 1963. 36p.

International Commission of Jurists. Cuba and the rule of law. Geneva. 1962. 267p.

Kosta, V. La révolution cubaine et ses repércussions internationales. Oct. 20, 1962. 13 (301) Rev. Politique Internationale (Belgrade) 6-8.

Lavergne, B. L'affaire de Cuba, l'action du president Kennedy. Le rôle prochain de l'O.N.U. 1962. 34 Ann. Politique et Economique 315-38.

Mallison, W. T., Jr. Limited naval blockade or quarantine—interdiction: national and collective defense claims valid under international law. 1962. 31 Geo. Wash. L. Rev. 335-98.

Maza Rodríguez, E. Castro, la revolución cubana y la autodeterminación de los pueblos. Julio-Agosto 1962. Revista Estudios Políticos 175-90.

Mikoyan in Cuba; full texts of the speeches made by Anastas L. Mikoyan, first vice chairman of the USSR on his tour of Cuba Feb. 4-13, 1960. New York, Crosscurrents Press. 1960. 88p.

Monahan, James and Gilmore, K. O. The great deception; the inside story of how the Kremlin took over Cuba. New York, Farrar, Strauss. 1963. 213p.

Montague, R. L., III. A brief study of some of the international legal and political aspects of the Guantanamo Bay problem. 1962. 50 Ky. L. J. 459-522.

Morray, James P. The second revolution in Cuba, New York, Monthly Review Press. 1962. 173p.

Oliver, Covey. International law and the quarantine of Cuba. 1963. 57 Am. J. Int'l L. 373-7.

Pachter, Henry M. American-Soviet confrontation; a case study of the Cuban missile crisis. New York, Praeger. 1963.

Phillips, Ruby. The Cuban dilemma. New York, Obolensky. 1963. 357p.

Reeves, W. H. Cuban situation: the political and economic relations of the United States and Cuba. 1962. 17 Bus. Law. 980-96.

Rodríguez Morejón, Gerardo. Fidel Castro, biografía. Habana, P. Fernández. 1959. 259p.

Romero Carranza, Ambrosio. Excepciones legítimas y legales al principio de no intervención. Sept./Oct. 1961. Jurisprudencia Argentina (1961-V-sec. doct. pp. 39-45).

Ronning, C. Neale. Law and politics in inter-American diplomacy. New York, Wiley. 1963.

Schmitt, Karl M. and Burks, David D. Evolution or chaos: dynamics of Latin American government and politics. New York, Praeger. 1963.

Seligman, Eustace. Legality of U.S. quarantine action under the United Nations charter. 1963. 49 A. B. A. J. 142-5.

Szulc, Tad. The winds of revolution: Latin America today—and tomorrow. New York, Praeger. 1963.

Taber, Robert. M-26; biography of a revolution. New York, Lyle Stuart. 1961. 348p.

Tang, Peter S. H. and Maloney, J. The Chinese Communist impact on Cuba. Chestnut Hill, Mass. 1962. 125p. (Research Institute on the Sino-Soviet Bloc. Monograph series 12).

United States. Dep't of Defense. Armed forces information and education. Cuba: questions and answers. Washington, Gov't Print. Off. 1962. 28p. (DOD-GEN-2).

United States. Presidential proclamation no. 3504 on interdiction of the delivery of offensive weapons to Cuba. Oct. 23, 1962. 1963. 57 Am. J. Int'l L. 512-13.

Velasco Gil, Carlos M. Cuba sí! Yanquis no! México. 1960. 310p.

Williams, William A. The United States, Cuba and Castro; an essay on the dynamics of revolution and the dissolution of empire. New York, Monthly Review Press. 1962. 179p.

NOTES

NOTES
TO
WORKING PAPER ON THE INTER-AMERICAN SECURITY
SYSTEM AND THE CUBAN CRISIS

[1] MECHAM, THE UNITED STATES AND INTER-AMERICAN SECURITY 1889-1960, 481 (1961). Throughout the preparation of this paper my task has been lightened and my perspectives aided by this thorough and scholarly book, written by my one-time teacher of United States-Latin-American relations.

[2] So did some key figures in the XIXth century public life of the United States: "While Blaine seemed to see in the Pacific an American sphere of influence that must be protected, he was far more interested in his policy of Pan-Americanism than in any other phase of diplomacy. His dream, borrowed no doubt from Henry Clay whom he admired and imitated, was to induce the Latin-American states of North and South America to enter a kind of informal federation, with the United States, as an interested and friendly 'elder sister,' at its head." HICKS, THE AMERICAN NATION 303 (1946 printing).

[3] In his note of July 20, 1895, to Lord Salisbury on the matter of the boundary dispute between Venezuela and Great Britain over the boundary with British Guiana: "Today the United States is practically sovereign on this continent, and its fiat is law upon the subjects to which it confines its interposition."

[4] For a judgment to the effect that the danger was largely illusory, see PERKINS, A HISTORY OF THE MONROE DOCTRINE 379 (1955).

[5] From the title to Chapter VII, id. at 229.

[6] By the "Bucarelli Agreement," which takes its name from the street location in Mexico City of the house where the conditions precedent to United States recognition of the Obregón Government were negotiated. See, generally, SEPULVEDA, LA TEORIA Y LA PRACTICA DEL RECONOCIMIENTO DE GOBIERNOS (1954).

[7] PERKINS, op. cit. supra note 4, at 343.

[8] Ibid.

[9] Convention on Rights and Duties of States, signed at Montevideo, December 26, 1933; entered into force for the United States, December 26, 1934. 49 Stat. 3097; 165 LNTS 19. Secretary Hull made a reservation at signature, calling attention to the need for definition and interpretation of fundamental terms used in the Convention but pledging the Roosevelt administration ". . . to follow scrupulously the doctrines and policies which it has pursued since March 4th . . ." as embodied in addresses of President Roosevelt and in

the "peace address" of Secretary Hull. As to the lack of effect of this reservation on the issue of intervention, because of a later statement of President Roosevelt, see MECHAM, *op. cit. supra* note 1, at 116.

[10] It is puzzling that, although the recognition problem in the Americas has always been that of recognition of revolutionary *governments*, the Convention deals with the recognition of *states*. As to the difference between recognition of entities as states and of regimes as governments, see AMERICAN LAW INSTITUTE, RESTATEMENT OF THE LAW: THE FOREIGN RELATIONS LAW OF THE UNITED STATES §§97,98 (Proposed Official Draft, 1962).

[11] The Eighth International Conference of American States, December 9-27, 1938. The Declaration of Lima was not a treaty and hence is not carried in the official records of international agreements. Final acts of this character are reported in the Department of State Bulletin (from 1939 on) and in secondary sources.

[12] First Meeting of Consultation of the Ministers of Foreign Affairs of the American Republics, Panamá, September 23—October 3, 1939. The acts and declarations of this Conference are not carried in TREATIES IN FORCE, January 1, 1961. This Department of State publication lists treaties and other international agreements of the United States in force as of the time stated in any particular issue. It is a very useful research aid. For the text of the Declaration on the High Seas Zone, see I Dept. of State Bull. 331 (1939) and 7 HACKWORTH, INTERNATIONAL LAW 702 (1943).

[13] Second Meeting of Consultation of the Ministers of Foreign Affairs of the American Republics, Habana, July 21-30, 1940. Two international agreements resulted from this meeting: (i) Convention on the Provisional Administration of European Colonies and Possessions in the Americas, signed July 30, 1940; entered into force for the United States, January 8, 1942. 56 Stat. 1273; 161 UNTS 253. (ii) Act of Habana Concerning the Provisional Administration of European Colonies and Possessions in the Americas, signed July 30, 1940; entered into force for the United States, July 30, 1940. 54 Stat. 2491.

[14] Third Meeting of Consultation of the Ministers of Foreign Affairs of the American Republics, Rio de Janeiro, January 15-28, 1942. See MECHAM, *op. cit. supra* note 1, 210-245 on the cooperative arrangements made at Rio and their implementation during World War II.

[15] The original Article 21 was on a minor matter that was simply dropped out of the Covenant when the new Article was introduced.

[16] This conference was called, as an extraordinary meeting, by the United Mexican States. It is not one of the periodic series of inter-American conferences. It is reported in Report Submitted to the Governing Board of the Pan American Union by the Director General (1945); see also, Mann, "Elimination of Axis Influence in this

Hemisphere: Measures Adopted at the Mexico City Conference," XII Dept. of State Bull. 924 (1945).

[17] Inter-American Treaty of Reciprocal Assistance, opened for signature at Rio de Janeiro, September 2, 1947; entered into force for the United States, December 3, 1948, 62 Stat. 1681; 21 UNTS 79.

[18] Article 9-a. Under Article 9-b invasion of territory is aggression. Under Art. 9-a an unprovoked armed attack is aggression. This suggests the possibility that response to a provoked attack would not be aggression, if the response were not an invasion. The treaty does not make clear whether response to a provoked attack is limited to self-defense measures, or, what amounts to the same thing, whether "provocation" (not defined) may be something less than the type of overt hostile case that justifies self-defense.

[19] This phraseology seems to imply that North and South America are a single continent. This usage sometimes occurs in Spanish: "Blanda la faz, benigno el continente, tal es la libertad."

[20] Charter of the Organization of American States, signed at Bogotá, April 30, 1948; entered into force for the United States, December 13, 1951. 2 UST 2394; 119 UNTS 3.

[21] The Montevideo formulation on recognition declared recognition to be ". . . unconditional and irrevocable." No such statement is made on Articles 9 and 10 of the Charter. This may have a bearing on the question whether recognition extended to a regime as a government may be made subject to a power to withdraw such recognition even though there is no other regime available to be recognized in its stead. Cf. note 10 and see RESTATEMENT, *id.* §99 (2).

[22] Oliver, book review, STONE, AGGRESSION AND WORLD ORDER, 108 U. Pa. L. Rev. 279 (1959).

[23] These statements, made to me in Spanish by Latin Americans, are fixed in my mind in Spanish and seem to lose some of their point in exact translation. Hence I have imposed them upon the reader of the text in the language in which I heard, and was troubled by, them. They mean (i) that we get too nervous about things we should be brave enough to endure; (ii) that we seem a little silly when we, with all our might, express fear of tiny countries (Guatemala, Cuba). The statements, of course, well preceded October 22, 1962.

[24] Inter-American Conferences [of States] are declared to be the supreme organ of the Organization of American States. See OAS Charter, Articles 32 and 33.

[25] The principal work of this Inter-American Conference was the Charter of the Organization of American States, *supra* note 19.

[26] The evolution of the Declaration of Caracas can be traced in the report in XXX Dept. of State Bull. 419-426, (1954). The text of the Declaration is at 420, *id.*

[27] Apparently this Committee was made up of the Foreign Ministers and no reference of its work to a plenary session was considered necessary.

[28] It is not carried in Treaties in Force, *op. cit. supra* note 12, as an international agreement of the United States. As to the distinction between international agreements and declarations on matters of common policy not intended to create, change or define relationships under the international law, see Restatement, *op. cit. supra* note 10, §118, *Comment f.*

[29] Mecham, *op. cit. supra* note 1:444,470 (citing Yepes, a leading Latin-American authority on Pan Americanism as being in accord).

[30] This was written before October 22, 1962, with the referrals to the United Nations made by the Arbenz regime in 1954 and by the Castro regime, 1960-62, in mind. Events after October 22, 1962, have made the statement almost *a fortiori.*

[31] United Nations practice links "dispute-peaceful settlement-Chapter VI." It is in this area that the Security Council is clearly obliged to "encourage . . . pacific settlement of local disputes through . . . regional arrangements," Article 52-3.

[32] Although "dispute" and "situation" appear to be used on an equal footing in Chapter VI, with the Security Council having the power to investigate either to determine ". . . whether the continuance of the dispute or situation is likely to endanger the maintenance of international peace and security" [article 34], in practice the term "situation" is linked to threats to peace, breaches of the peace and aggression under Chapter VII, probably because of the use of the term in Article 40, providing for provisional measures [of enforcement action] to prevent ". . . an aggravation of the situation." At any rate, the Guatemalan delegate based his argument in large part on the premise that, as there was no "dispute" with Honduras, Chapter VI did not apply and hence no reference to the OAS should be made.

[33] The United Nations Official Records/Security Council, 9th Year, 675th and 676th Meetings do not report the exact words used by Mr. Lodge; but see XXXI Dept. of State Bull. 28 (1954), indicating that he warned the U.S.S.R. to ". . . stay out of this hemisphere." The quotations from the Soviet delegate in the outline are abridged from remarks at pages 32 and 34 of the Record of the 675th meeting.

[34] After the Brazilian-Colombian resolution was lost on a vote of 10 for (Brazil, China, Colombia, Denmark, France, Lebanon, New Zealand, Turkey, United Kingdom, United States) to 1 against (U.S.S.R.), the French delegate proposed the following resolution, which was adopted unanimously:

"*The Security Council,*

"*Having considered* on an urgent basis the communication of the Government of Guatemala to the President of the Security Council (S/3232),

"*Calls* for the immediate termination of any action likely to cause bloodshed and requests all Members of the United Nations to abstain, in the spirit of the Charter, from rendering assistance to any such action." [Official Records, 675th Meeting, p. 38.]

The Soviet Union and Guatemala called for another session, pressing new evidence supporting the case for United Nations action, despite the fact that the Inter-American Peace Committee had informed the Council that a commission of inquiry had been established to proceed to Central America to deal with the question. At the 676th Meeting, June 25, 1954, there was a procedural wrangle, much discussion (despite the fact that the issue was adoption of the agenda) of the relationship between the OAS and the UN. The agenda for the meeting failed by 5 votes against adoption (Brazil, China, Colombia, Turkey, United States) to 4 for adoption (Denmark, Lebanon, New Zealand, U.S.S.R.), with 2 abstentions (France and the United Kingdom). The Arbenz regime collapsed on June 27. The subcommittee of the Inter-American Peace Committee began its trip to Central America on June 29 but got no farther than Mexico City, because the new regime in Guatemala advised against continuing, MECHAM, *op. cit. supra* note 1, 451. On the face of it, the record leaves open the possibility that the failure of the UN to act and the *de facto* referral to the Inter-American Peace Committee gave the "invaders" time to complete their work, and this was one major cause of the "veritable hornets' nest of criticism of the United States" that followed. See MECHAM, *ibid.*

[35] MECHAM, *id.* at 446, discusses the opposition within Guatemala to the Arbenz regime by army officers once the plan to equip a people's militia came to light. [The Arbenz regime is not the only regime in Latin America to have felt the opposition of the officer corps to the creation and arming of potentially rival establishments.]

[36] This meeting of the Foreign Ministers as the Organ of Consultation, August 16-28, 1960, was initiated through the Council of the OAS as a result of charges of aggression and intervention brought by Venezuela against Castro Cuba. In voting for the convocation the United States representative to the OAS Council said:

"There are, in the opinion of my Government, other and very serious matters which also require the urgent consideration of the American governments at this time . . . Outstanding among these matters is the growing evidence of the desire of the Soviet Union to intervene more directly in the affairs of this hemisphere. The threat of missile warfare made by Chairman Khrushchev on July 9 is but the most spectacular example of the effort of the Soviet Union to exert an increasing influence upon the relations of the American Republics." (XLIII Dept. of State Bull. 225 [August 8, 1960].)

The United States also presented to the Inter-American Peace Committee, August 2, 1960, a lengthy memorandum on the subject, "Responsibility of the Cuban Government for Increased International Tensions in the Hemisphere," *id.*, 317-346. Nonetheless, and despite a supplemental document submitted at San Jose by the United

States, as well as OAS Committee and Secretariat studies and reports, and the efforts of Secretary Herter there, the meeting accomplished little. The San Jose Conference is reported, *id.* 395-412; the Declaration is at 407.

[37] Uruguay, January 22-31, 1962. This was the "8th Meeting of Consultation of Ministers of Foreign Affairs, serving as the Organ of Consultation in Application of the Inter-American Treaty of Reciprocal Assistance." The Conference is reported in XLVI Dept. of State Bull., No. 1182, 267-288 (February 19, 1962). The text of the Resolutions is at *id.,* 278-282. See, also, Report of Senators Morse and Hickenlooper to the Committee on Foreign Relations, 87th Cong., 2d Sess., March, 1962. For an analysis of the legal situation after the quite qualified success of the Conference, see Fenwick, Editorial: "The Issues at Punta del Este: Non-Intervention v. Collective Security," 56 Am. J. Int'l Law 469 (1962).

[38] Resolution VII, XLVI Dept. of State Bull. 281 (February 19, 1962).

[39] Resolution IX, *id.* 282.

[40] The Article provides: "Amendments to the present Charter may be adopted only at an Inter-American Conference convened for that purpose. Amendments shall enter into force in accordance with the terms and procedure set forth in Article 109" [entry into force when two-thirds of the signatories have deposited ratifications].

[41] Resolution VI, *op. cit. supra* note 38, 281.

[42] XLVII Dept. of State Bull. 541 (No. 1215, October 8, 1962).

[43] *New York Times,* October 23, 1962, p. 18.

[44] My phrase, coined for lawyers, not the President's. I have remarked elsewhere that, of course, this is another "unruly horse" that presents the difficulty of where you will be carried if you mount. Pushed to an extreme anticipatory self-defense is aggression.

[45] Emphasis added.

[46] *New York Times,* October 24, 1962, p. 22.

[47] See note 20, *supra.*